Thank God It's Monday

Thank God It's Monday

Patrick Klingaman

 VICTOR BOOKS

A DIVISION OF SCRIPTURE PRESS PUBLICATIONS INC.
USA   CANADA   ENGLAND

Copyediting: Afton Rorvik
Cover Design: Scott Rattray

ISBN:1-56476-538-5

1 2 3 4 5 6 7 8 9 10 Printing/Year 00 99 98 97 96

C o n t e n t s

Dedication

To my mother, Mary Elizabeth Klingaman, who found something to love in whatever I wrote, just because it came from her son.

Acknowledgments

When a book project is completed, it is natural for its author to be thankful to many people for many reasons. Above all, I give thanks to God for placing within me the desire to write and for helping me see the need to tell others about the ministry of everyday work. I am grateful to my father, Forrest Klingaman, for providing my first positive role model in the business world. Without the unwavering encouragement of my wife, Kathy, I might not have had the persistence to keep this book alive when it was still largely an idea and a bunch of bulging file folders. She has become a great partner in this ministry, teaching women about work and applying God's Word to her own job better than anyone else I know.

Thanks to Stephen Schmitz, who was involved in many late-night brainstorming sessions during the inception of this book idea. And to Roger Green at HealthEast, whose willingness to restructure my job gave me the extra writing time I needed. I am grateful to editors who encouraged me to pursue this topic early on: Bill Deckard, Nathan Unseth, and Greg Pierce. At Victor Books, I thank David Horton for his wise guidance and for believing in this project. Readers can join me in thanking Afton Rorvik for her skillful copyediting. She has a gift for finding muddy sentences and making them read clearly. I was also blessed by fellow writers' critique group members Kirk Livingston, Jerry Sedgewick, and Patty Thomson, who were first to read many of the chapters and offered great suggestions for improvement. Finally, I'd like to thank those who allowed me to interview them, or who took classes from me. Sharing their experiences with me broadened my point of view and helped make my writing relevant to a greater number of people.

1

A Marketplace That Needs God

Those of us who are both Christians and employees often face conflict in living out those two roles.

In my role as a Christian, I struggle with finding much time for traditional ministry activities. After nine or more hours of meetings, deadlines, and brain-testing projects, some days all I can manage to do is go home, eat dinner, stare at the television, and fall asleep while reading the Bible. Weekends are filled with household projects I didn't have the energy to complete during the week, spending time with my wife, and a smattering of social obligations.

Sundays are better, as I am uplifted while I worship and listen to the sermon. Yet, as I look through the church program, I am often frustrated at all the ministry opportunities available. Frustrated because I can't seem to find time to take advantage of half of what I feel I ought to. Shouldn't God take first priority? I could sign up for that in-depth Bible study, but when would I find the time to study, especially since we're shorthanded at work? I feel a strong need to be an active, vital part of God's ministry, but I'm not always sure how to fit it into my hectic life. Boy, if only I didn't have to work for a living. Then I could really serve God!

Most of my waking hours are spent in my other role as a businessman. Here, the conflict is trying to compete successfully in business without compromising my Christian principles. Even as a student studying for my M.B.A. with would-be business leaders, I saw signs that made me wonder how well I'd fit into the business world.

❏ For many students, class work became secondary to getting a good job. One classmate was too busy traveling to interviews to keep up with his homework, so he offered others money to include his name on a group project for which he did no work.

❏ I did not have a problem with the placement office's instruction to look, act, and speak like a person companies would want to hire—until I had interviews with a firm whose largest division manufactures cigarettes and an ad agency with a large tobacco company as a client. I was too lost in the flurry of activity aimed at landing me a job, to screen out companies I didn't want to work for. While I was trying to sell myself during those particular interviews, however, I kept visualizing all the deceiving magazine ads that depict smoking as cool. Could I really feel proud coming up with the equivalent of the next Joe Camel promotion? Although I did not dismiss myself from the interviews, I think my "hire me" pitch lacked conviction. Neither firm made me a job offer.

❏ The biggest measure of success in my graduating class was not one's grades but the heft of one's starting salary. So great was the desire to succeed in this area that some students kept flying off to interviews even after they had accepted a lucrative job offer. After all, another company might top their current offer by $1,000 or so. Should that happen, they would simply back out of their employment agreement, sometimes just a few weeks before they were supposed to begin work.

After this disturbing preview of the business world, I wondered if I could hold my own in an anything-goes marketplace when there are certain anythings I wouldn't do—tactics others appeared to be using to their advantage. Would a turn-the-other-cheek approach turn me into the office doormat? Should I model my behavior more after Samson than after Christ, beating those infidels at their own game?

Christians As Roses in the Workplace

Ideally, we wouldn't have to face such conflicts. The business world would be a wonderful place to work, an environment well-suited for service to God. Companies would strive to produce products and services of the highest quality, and their customers would almost always be satisfied. Workers at all levels would understand the importance of their task to the organization, taking pride in their company and in a job well done. They would work diligently for their bosses, as if working for the Lord. Each work task throughout the day would be as an offering to God; simple, yet pleasing. Because of that attitude, Christians would be known as being among the hardest working and best workers around. Their character and acts would shine as an example to all, and there would be many an eager ear straining to hear their "secret." Sharing their faith would flow naturally out of this, and many souls would be won to Christ. Increasingly, others would seek to start their own businesses to meet unfulfilled needs in the community, provide more good jobs, and serve God through their honest efforts.

Sounds appealing, doesn't it? Unfortunately, it doesn't smack of reality. The real world we work in and read about is not so pretty.

❑ Because of a rash of hostile takeover attempts, the 1980s have been coined "the greed decade" in some business circles. In that ten-year period $1.5 trillion in corporate assets were turned over in takeovers that made those involved in corporate raiding rich (for example, KKR's buyout of RJR Nabisco produced $760 million in fees for lawyers, investment bankers, and commercial banks), but left many companies reeling in debt and made the market for junk bonds shaky. [1]

❑ Those who didn't make enough millions in the takeovers themselves made some extra cash buying and selling stocks, based on insider information. Two of the most visible players in the insider trading scandal, Ivan Boesky and Michael Milken, agreed to pay back a combined total of $700 million in illegal profits. [2]

❑ Homicide has become the second leading cause of death on the job, as disgruntled or dismissed employees express their anger with bullets instead of words. The most dangerous occupations for being murdered are: sales clerks, service occupation workers, and executives/managers in sales and service industries. [3]

❏ A television news story showed K Mart officials being accused of forcing out long-term managers by creating negative performance reviews and subsequent demotions. The reason: affected managers said it was a corporate strategy to trim down management payroll by replacing older managers with younger, lower-paid personnel. Other firms have also been accused of using this sort of cost-cutting approach.

❏ It is common knowledge in the retail field that more theft is committed by employees than shoplifters. One store owner installed a video camera, which showed sales clerks not ringing up many purchases on the cash register and slipping the bills into their pockets.

In such an environment, one would think that Christians would stand out like red roses in Antarctica. In my experience, I've had to look hard to find very many roses in the workplace. Too often we soften our colors to blend in with those around us. In fact, during my long tenure in a healthcare organization with over 5,000 employees, I wouldn't have known of any Christians outside my department if it hadn't been for occasional religious events like prayer breakfasts and Bible studies. Christians I know in other companies large and small express similar frustrations and feelings of isolation.

Despite the often bleak realities, encouraging signs are appearing both in the business world and in Christian circles. Top business authors like Tom Peters (*In Search of Excellence* and *Liberation Management*) and Kenneth Blanchard (*The One Minute Manager* and *The Power of Ethical Management*) have challenged the ruthless, tough-guy image of business success. The new model of good business practice involves genuine caring for customers, employees, and even the environment. Key traits that innovative companies are valuing most in their leaders include honesty, integrity, being a supporter/encourager, and being a creator of positive company values and vision. As more organizations and managers adopt this new model, the marketplace should become a more enjoyable place to work.

Looking at the universal church shows some positive trends as well. Worldwide, the number of Christians is growing. Also, recent Christian involvement in political issues such as abortion and world hunger may indicate that believers seem less willing to confine their spirituality to within church walls on Sunday. The section in Christian bookstores on "applied Christianity" seems to be bursting with new titles, helping readers apply their faith in areas such as relationships, parenting, education, politics, sexuality, and even employment.

Those of us who are Christians working in business would do well to find a way to merge these two trends. I still remember the impact of a statement made by a speaker at a corporate mission month activity years ago. She referred to the two "excellence" books coauthored by Tom Peters (*In Search of Excellence* and *A Passion for Excellence*) as handbooks of Christian management principles. Even though those volumes make no mention of God, the main theme of being fully committed to serving your customers and taking care of your employees seems to fit quite well with Christ's command for us to serve one another in love.

Think about the possibilities! We could perform the majority of our business tasks with zeal, knowing our service will help the company's bottom line and be consistent with the principles of our faith. Also, much of our desire to serve Christ could be fulfilled as we spread God's love through our many hours of work in the marketplace. Those wishful thoughts of being involved in "full-time" ministry could come true for most of us without quitting our jobs and enrolling in seminary.

Barriers to a Spiritual Connection with Work

Despite these exciting possibilities, most of us continually struggle with making a positive spiritual connection with our work. Until we identify and overcome our barriers to making that connection, we as Christians will have difficulty making a real impact in the business sector for God. I see five obstacles that hold us back.

> **Most of us continually struggle with making a positive spiritual connection with our work.**

1. Christians have been given little training in applying biblical principles to the workplace. How many sermons have you heard concerning work? In my own church experience, I can recall two such sermons—one of which I delivered myself! Considering most of us spend about half our waking hours working, work commands a disproportionately small amount of sermon, Sunday School, and religious reading time. When I consider the wealth of Christian resources available on parenting or building a happy marriage, the resources available for those of us in the work world look pretty sparse. I've had to aggressively hunt down good resources for applying my faith in the business world, requiring greater use of my market research skills than it should have.

Why the shortage of good resources? Most sermons, Sunday School studies, seminars, and books are prepared by ministers, priests, and others involved in "full-time ministry." Few have spent much time in the business world, making it difficult to teach on the subject from any personal experience. They are quite naturally drawn toward teaching what they do know: the Bible, personal spirituality, and relationship building. Teaching on work, therefore, occurs infrequently and, when it does happen, is often too general to be directly applicable.

Adequate spiritual training for people in business will not occur if we rely solely on professional ministers and ministries to do the job. Wise and experienced Christian business leaders need to emerge and play a larger role in training other business professionals.

The desperate need for such training was made clear at a "Your Work Matters to God" workshop put on by Doug Sherman of Career Impact Ministries. Several hundred people from all over the Minneapolis/St. Paul area attended. Some were very successful executives, many were long-time Christians who hold positions of leadership in churches. One aspect of the event that struck me was the excitement created in the room by a simple message that God cares about our everyday work because work has spiritual value. Many in the audience had never heard this kind of teaching before and were fired up by it. It made me wonder how many others are out there who have not been exposed to what God's Word says about work.

The title of the conference shows just how far Christianity has strayed from the daily grind: "Your Work Matters to God." In any other aspect of our faith, such a title might seem too simplistic. Imagine signing up for workshops like these: "Your Family Matters to God," "God Wants You to Pray," "Church Work Can Be Ministry."

2. *Worldly principles have deceived Christians.* Without adequate knowledge of biblical principles related to business and work, it is easy for Christians to be influenced by worldly business views. I call the two most common worldly views that some Christians hold *The Jungle* and The *Candy Store*.

Those holding *The Jungle* view see the business world as a wild and cutthroat place, where only the toughest survive. Nice guys finish last in this world. They would say "a dog-eat-dog business world is no place for lambs." *Do unto others before they do unto you* is a chief commandment.

Businesspeople with this view will obviously have a hard time applying Christ's teaching on the job. To them, mixing God with business is a recipe for financial failure. Too much "love thy enemy" stuff could cause them to lose their competitive edge. They see being Christlike at work and being successful as mutually exclusive career choices—and they don't want to be failures. That leads to a kind of "Sunday Christianity," illustrated at its most extreme in movies about the Mafia and organized crime. Mafia bosses are shown piously worshiping in church on Sunday and issuing a contract to "rub someone out" on Monday. Business is business, you know.

An industrial company I know of had a "tough-guy" manager like this. He was gruff and autocratic, never truly delegating responsibility to those under him. Although he could chew someone out for bad performance, he was unable to soften up enough to train, coach, and support his subordinates so they could improve. After efforts to get him to change his style in a couple different management positions, the company let him go.

The Candy Store is also a worldly business view, despite the fact that its proponents see things exactly the opposite of those holding *The Jungle* view. Here, the world is like the candy store I remember from childhood. I would walk in holding Mom's or Dad's hand and point to whatever candy I wanted. The lady behind the glass counter would carefully pick out just the right piece with her plastic-gloved hand, drop it in a bag, and it would be mine. On shopping excursions, I gradually learned that, if I behaved myself all day, chances were pretty good my parents would treat me to whatever sweets I wanted (within reason, of course).

Candy Store Christians liken the world to that candy store, with God being the wealthiest dad in town. Ask God for that vice-president's position, a million-dollar house, or an explosively growing business. He'll provide that and more if you have enough faith. Believe in God with all your heart, and you'll be blessed with a long life and riches like Abraham and Solomon. Those with *The Candy Store* view call it a "prosperity gospel," a concept based on misinterpretations and exaggerations of biblical passages. (I'll discuss this further in chapter 11.) In a nutshell, they take a good concept (praying to God) and give it an improper motive (financial gain). Business success becomes a triumph of faith; failure a result of sin and doubt. *Candy Store* Christians can't conceive that God's will for what's best for them doesn't always include riches, worldly success, and good health. They believe everything behind life's glass counter is there just waiting for us to ask for it.

Jim Bever, owner of a landscaping business, is a good argument against *The Candy Store* theory. When I think of godly men who make their work a ministry, Jim is one of the first I think of. Yet, twice his business has struggled and put him under a load of heavy debt—enough to make most people run toward bankruptcy. Each time he has dug out of debt and earned a lot of respect from others in the process. He prays for his business—as do others—and God has used it, blessed it, and brought others to Christ through it. God has not chosen to make Jim rich by our society's standard, but I'm quite sure he prefers God's other blessings to the money.

3. Some view the business world as an adversary. People who view the business world as an evil adversary share *The Jungle* view of business, but with one exception. They don't want to live by jungle rules. That leaves them with two options: fight or flight. They either reject business as too worldly an occupation or fight to rid the field of sin. Neither approach makes much of an impact for Christ.

I have a friend who used to sell computer systems and grew to despise nearly every aspect of that job. He disliked the traveling, the intense pressure from bosses to close the sale, and the company approach to moving up the corporate ladder, which involved uprooting every few years and moving to another part of the country. For awhile, his impulse was to leave his job behind and do something dramatic, like entering a monastery. He needed to find some spiritual meaning in his life, yet he couldn't conceive of finding it on the treadmill of work he was running on. Eventually, he decided to search, not for a total escape, but for a career better suited to his interests and abilities.

Staying in the fray is important to God. If good people reject business as a career because of its perceived evil, immorality in the field will only worsen. We need to understand that business itself is not sinful or corrupt but, like any human-run institution, it has sinful people working for it.

> **If good people reject business as a career because of Its perceived evil, immorality in the field will only worsen.**

Some Christians not only stay in the fray but try to rid industry of sin single-handedly. We need to be responsible for our own sinful behavior and, to a certain degree, the proper work conduct of those reporting to us. Yet sometimes our hatred of sin and desire for righteousness can lead us to extend our reach too far.

I know of an owner of a chain of health clubs who was known as a strong Christian and ran his business with integrity. One day newspaper reports surfaced with employees accusing the owner of religious discrimination. They claimed their employer tried to control not only their conduct at work, but also their lives off the job. A righteous lifestyle was becoming a factor in hiring, promoting, and disciplining employees, according to the news stories. Lawsuits followed and the man is no longer in business. I'm sure he was motivated from his love of God and hatred of sin, yet he was perhaps trying to manage the unmanageable. At best, those of us who are managers can inspire our employees to work hard and work well. We can't create a work environment free of sin or sinners. That's a job reserved for Christ alone.

4. Ministry at work is often seen as limited to evangelism and charitable contributions. Work itself has no ministry value, according to many Christians I've talked to. They—particularly those with a more evangelical outlook—believe that the value of work lies in bringing us in touch with unbelievers so we can witness to them. The money we make at work also enables us to support ministry through our contributions. Although both of these are important tasks (which will be addressed in future chapters), neither relate to the actual act of working.

In my own case, I've found that approach to be very limiting and not fulfilling. Even though I am certainly not close-lipped when it comes to sharing my faith, only a small fraction of my workday includes activities I would classify as evangelism. Hardly enough for me to consider my job a ministry. I found it disturbing to think that my work might matter only in how it impacted others spiritually. If I shut my office door to finish a last-minute project, have I closed down my ministry for the day? What about those people who conduct their business out of the home? Is their ministry limited to witnessing to the mail carrier and phone solicitors?

This restricted view of ministry is dangerous because it limits our perception of how valuable we are in God's kingdom. In my own case, adding up the periodic opportunities to share my faith with the few thousand dollars I was able to give away each year hardly made me feel as if I was on the cutting edge of God's ministry. It seemed as if I were wasting a lot of time doing tasks that didn't matter to God.

5. Committed Christians often save their best for church and other formal ministries. When Christ enters the heart of a sinner, He creates a heart that desires to please Him. Part of that desire is to share in Christ's ministry on earth. Because many Christians don't see work as a well-defined ministry, much of our spiritual zeal and energy is diverted into more concrete ministries such as church service. Few activities are more important than supporting our local church body, but limiting our "ministry" to that can really constrict our ability to serve God.

My first heavy involvement in church ministry began after I received my M.B.A. and settled down in Minnesota. I became quite involved in my church singles congregation, leading Bible study groups, organizing and assisting in social activities (i.e., fellowship with the opposite sex), teaching, and even editing an elaborate singles newsletter. For the first time in my life, I really felt God using me and my abilities for His kingdom.

This service to God was a source of real fulfillment, yet it also brought great frustration. I felt as if I should be able to do more for God, but there was a shortage of time to do it. After work and other obligations, I found it difficult to handle much more than ten to fifteen hours of church activities per week without beginning to feel signs of burnout. *Surely God deserves more than ten hours a week,* I thought. Boy, if I just didn't have to work for a living; then I could really serve God! In my eyes, work became a hindrance to ministry. I poured so much time and energy into Bible study and church activities that my job performance turned mediocre. The job got done but my work lacked freshness and creativity. I was going through the motions for 40 hours a week so I had the energy to do church ministry during my off-hours.

I wonder how many Christians are struggling as I was, seeing work as a necessary evil or, at best, a lower level of ministry than "religious" service? Many friends and fellow churchgoers I've talked to share at least some of these views and frustrations. My greatest concern is that the marketplace is being neglected by committed Christians. If we don't strive for excellence in the business world, Christians will be severely underrepresented among top business leaders—those executives with the greatest potential to make a profound impact on society.

I believe all five of these obstacles have blocked and limited our impact as Christians in the business world. What we need is a broader understanding of what ministry is, as well as guidelines for applying that to our day-to-day business activities. We need to move our discussions beyond the business ethics debates of what is right or wrong. Being Christ's servants in business requires us first to look at how we approach our work because actions (right or wrong) flow from our attitudes.

> **My greatest concern is that the marketplace is being neglected by committed Christians.**

This book is divided into three sections. Part One builds the case for seeing business as a legitimate ministry, serving both God and man. Part Two outlines a number of key biblical principles relating to work and business—wisdom that makes business sense. Finally, in Part Three I address a number of challenging issues Christians face in business, such as dealing with success, money, and entrepreneurial ambitions. In the appendix I have included questions suitable for a small group discussion.

This book does not attempt to break new theological ground. Several good studies into the theology of work have been completed in recent years, providing me a solid, biblically sound base from which to operate. Here, I seek to apply that teaching to everyday business life. In my studies, I found a surprising amount of overlap between how the Bible tells us to work and what some of today's executive experts tell us are sound management strategies. I was encouraged to discover so many areas where I could potentially please both my employer and God. Excellence in business does not have to come at the cost of spiritual impoverishment. If we commit our work to God and apply God's wisdom to our work, we can make a lasting impact on today's business world.

Think about It

❏   In your own life and work, can you think of any obstacles that keep you from serving God as much as you desire?

❏   What are the spiritual needs where you work?

Notes:

1. Josh Eppinger, "The Greed Decade," *Adweek's Marketing Week* (15 January 1990): 20–27.
2. James B. Stewart, *Den of Thieves* (New York: Simon & Schuster, 1991), 16.
3. Gene Meyer, "Warning: Work Can Be Hazardous to Your Health," *Minneapolis Star Tribune* (21 November 1993): 1J.

*Part*1
Seeing Business as Ministry

Ten years ago, if I had come across a book with the subtitle, "Making Business Your Ministry," I would've been surprised—and curious to figure out why anyone would use the terms *business* and *ministry* together. After all, business deals with money and ministry deals with souls, right?

To clearly see how work and business activities can become real ministry, we need to define terms and build a common foundation, answering questions such as:

❑ What is ministry?

❑ What is work and why is it important?

❑ What is God's work?

❑ How does God work with and through people?

❑ What work has God prepared me for?

I hope you find the following four chapters helpful in providing biblical answers to these questions, plus a few more.

2

Expand Your Concept of Ministry

S ome days, it is hard to imagine anything further from ministry than what happens at work. How many Monday mornings do most of us leap out of bed shouting, "Thank God it's
Monday. I get to go to work to serve God"? Instead, Mondays are
often the reason most of us thank God for Fridays, when the work
week is over.

Maybe you've had a Monday that went like this. You roll over
and stare at your alarm clock, hitting the snooze button. Gradually
your eyes focus on the clock, and you realize you have just enough
time to dress and run out the door. No coffee this morning.

Late Friday afternoon the boss threw everyone's schedule back
with a last-minute project, so now you have just enough time to prepare for the big afternoon meeting. You check your messages and
discover a panic call from a top executive with a problem that can't
wait. After playing telephone tag with all the various parties
required to put out that fire, you now have a lunch hour to prepare
for the meeting. And everyone who could help copy your handouts
has left early for lunch.

The meeting time arrives. The boss enters the boardroom and
makes a brief announcement: "Earnings have dipped and any presentations for new projects would be pointless."

Happy Monday!

On days like this it seems impossible to see business as ministry.
We just trudge along, muttering something about the curse of work
(sweat of the brow and all that). Despite such difficult days, most of

my problem with seeing business as ministry had nothing to do with the nature of the workplace. It had to do with my definition of ministry.

It wasn't too many years ago that I shared the world's more conventional view of ministry. Ministry is primarily the "godly stuff" that priests, missionaries, and other professional ministers do. It includes preaching, teaching, evangelism, and other spiritual tasks. As laypeople, we can help in this ministry through service in our church and by sharing the Gospel with those around us.

In recent years, my studies in the New Testament have revealed a dramatically different picture of ministry. New Testament writers don't distinguish between religious and secular work as we do. Our service to God is not limited to preaching the Gospel and helping in the church body. Rather, the Bible teaches us to do *everything* for God: "And whatever you do, whether in word or deed, do it all in the name of the Lord Jesus, giving thanks to God the Father through Him" (Col. 3:17).

> **New Testament writers don't distinguish between religious and secular work as we do.**

In that same chapter, Paul instructs slaves to serve their earthly masters as if working for the Lord. Those of us who need to work for others for our livelihood have much in common with those ancient slaves. Like them, we often answer to unreasonable bosses (masters) and work under less than ideal circumstances. Thus, Paul's teachings in verses 23 and 24 should apply to all workers:

> Whatever you do, work at it with all your heart, as working for the Lord, not for men, since you know that you will receive an inheritance from the Lord as a reward. It is the Lord Christ you are serving.

Phase One: Work As Duty

Transferring this original vision of ministry to my position in marketing did not occur all at once. The change happened in three distinct phases of thinking. The first phase I call the "work is my duty" phase. I knew I needed to work because it is something God commands us to do (and I need to eat). Paul urged early Christians to "do something useful" with their hands, so they could provide for themselves and others (Eph. 4:28; 1 Tim; 5:8).

Working to avoid becoming a sluggard, although a step in the right direction, hardly made for an inspiring approach to my job. I approached work about as gleefully as I approached mowing the lawn when I was a teenager. I mowed the lawn only because my father asked me to (repeatedly). I certainly had many things I'd rather spend my time doing, but I needed to obey my father.

It is important for us to understand that the vast majority of the people we work with each day are firmly entrenched in this phase. Many are waiting for that lucky lottery number or for the Publishers' Clearinghouse prize van to pull into their driveway so they can quit their jobs and live a life of leisure. In our office, when the lottery prize approaches $50 million, employees pool a few bucks each to buy a block of tickets. The pressure to throw your money away is great. If you don't contribute and the group wins, you'd be the only person left working in the department.

Phase Two: Work As Ministry Site

As I began to develop a little better understanding of the Bible, I moved on to my second phase of thinking. Here, my work world became a place where ministry could possibly occur. For example, others might notice the way I work and give me respect (1 Thes. 4:11-12).

Also, I discovered that the workplace is one of the best opportunities for Christians to share their faith. In Colossians 4:5, Paul encourages: "Be wise in the way you act toward outsiders; make the most of every opportunity." Few of us have more ongoing contact with "outsiders" than on the job. People are able to watch us day in and day out, noticing how we work, how we interact with others, and how we handle problems and conflict. Eventually, casual conversations with coworkers almost inevitably lead to some kind of opening to share our faith.

When I first moved back to Minnesota after graduate school, the only place I had any meaningful contact with non-Christians was at the office. After a ten-year absence, I had lost contact with all my childhood friends here. I lived in a large apartment complex with a rapid turnover of tenants, whom I rarely even bumped into in the hallways, much less developed relationships with. All my new friends were from church. My job became more valuable to me because it was the only place for me to practice meaningful evangelism.

God placed me in an ideal spiritual situation in my very first job out of school. I shared an office with a woman named Jeanne. Our desks were pushed together so we faced one another, giving us ample opportunity to talk. She seemed interested in spiritual matters and my church life, asking me lots of questions. Although I felt like a spiritual infant back then, I shared openly what Christ had done in my life. Jeanne had also struck up a friendship with another Christian guy in the building, so she probably talked more about religious topics than she ever had before.

Several months after leaving that job, Jeanne called me on the phone and told me she had made a commitment to Christ. Looking back, it was clear that God's plan was to place believers in the place Jeanne spent her days during her time of spiritual interest and decision. I felt God had wonderfully used me, although I strongly suspect I played a minor role compared to the other Christian who worked in the building. He became her husband.

Despite seeing the importance of sharing my faith at work, I still felt something was lacking. My work only seemed to matter to the extent that others were spiritually encouraged by it. Did it matter that I excelled at marketing our health care organization? I still didn't see a direct connection between my work duties and ministry.

Phase Three: Work As Ministry

The connection came as I entered my third phase of thinking—when I came to believe that work itself could be ministry. For starters, I learned that God Himself works, and He has given us the job of attending to His creation. In Genesis 1:28, God commands: "Be fruitful and increase in number; fill the earth and subdue it. Rule over the fish of the sea and the birds of the air and over every living creature that moves on the ground." Working in the world, therefore, is part of God's plan.

God has also blessed each of us with the gifts and abilities to carry out that work. Nowhere in the New Testament do we read that those identified spiritual gifts are our sole means for serving God. Besides those gifts, God has blessed each of us with inherent abilities and talents related to work. To some, He has given great mechanical aptitude; to others an analytical mind. Still others may have a natural compassion for others or a creative nature. God has so equipped us for a reason: to use and develop those gifts in a way that honors Him. If you seem to be skilled at working with numbers, becoming the best accountant or financial analyst you can may be a great way to serve God.

Using our natural abilities in our work sounds basic, but career experts estimate that at least half of those working are not in jobs suited to their primary interests and abilities. Those abilities become hidden and the world loses out as a result.

I know one person who has worked adequately in hospital finance for many years. One day he was part of a group giving a presentation on quality. When he stood up to instruct us on his topic, I was amazed at the transformation. He was full of energy, passion, and even creativity as a teacher. I was so impressed that I asked him to give a guest lecture on health care finance to a class I was teaching. There, he was even better. I know there is a shortage of truly exceptional teachers in all schools—and I believe this man had the abilities to be one of them.

So what is the value of using our abilities to serve God? All honest work done to honor God can contribute to the body of Christ. Look closely at the gifts of the body mentioned in Romans 12:4-8:

Just as each of us has one body with many members, and these members do not all have the same function, so in Christ we who are many form one body, and each member belongs to all the others. We have different gifts, according to the grace given us. If a man's gift is prophesying, let him use it in proportion to his faith. If it is serving, let him serve; if it is teaching, let him teach; if it is

> **All honest work done to honor God can contribute to the body of Christ.**

encouraging, let him encourage; if it is contributing to the needs of others, let him give generously; if it is leadership, let him govern diligently; if it is showing mercy, let him do it cheerfully.

How many of the above gifts can only be used in a church ministry setting? Except maybe for prophesying, any of these gifts can be used in all areas of our lives, including our work. In fact, one could argue that many of these gifts are necessary to become a great manager. Although executive greatness is still far from my grasp, I've noticed that I spend a good chunk of my workday serving, teaching, encouraging, giving, leading, and even showing mercy.

Sure, we can use those gifts on the job, but does that make it ministry? I don't think we should limit ministry to "spiritual" tasks because the actions of God Himself extend beyond the spiritual realm. Israel's exodus from Egypt was a result of a series of very tangible, physical acts of God, such as the plagues, the Passover, the parting of the Red Sea, and raining down manna for food. So our God is not just concerned with our spiritual welfare; He is concerned about the whole person. In Luke 12, Jesus tells us not to worry about what we will eat, drink, or wear. He will provide for those who "seek His kingdom."

God Works through Us

How does God provide for us? Spiritually, God provides the Holy Spirit, who acts in the lives of all Christians. Ask people how they came to know Christ, and they will often mention that God used the actions or words of another Christian to influence their decision for Christ.

God also provides for our material and physical needs through the actions of others. Sometimes that provision is directly through the output of one's work. Martin Luther once said that the way a cobbler loves his neighbor is by making good shoes. In addition to providing us with food, drink, and clothing, a successful business start-up will provide jobs for other families.

Is earnestly working to benefit others and provide for their physical needs a ministry comparable in importance to preaching the Gospel? The Bible doesn't clearly differentiate one type of ministry as being more important than another. It teaches that all the work of the body of Christ, all ministry, is important because it is all the work of God. Paul writes in 1 Corinthians 12:4-6: "There are different kinds of gifts, but the same Spirit. There are different kinds of service, but the same Lord. There are different kinds of working, but the same God works all of them in all men."

Work can be good ministry if we commit our work to God and allow Him to work through us. Working to provide for the physical needs of our family and others is important for two reasons. First, partly through our actions and those of other workers, God fulfills His promise in Luke 12:31 to provide for those who seek Him. Also, the provision of basic physical needs is often a prerequisite for a person being receptive to the Gospel. Missionaries in the Third World don't usually go to a village of starving people and simply preach. Their words would fall on deaf ears. First, they feed people and help meet life's most basic physical needs. Then spiritual needs can more readily be explored.

When I began looking at ministry from a broader perspective, I could see how my work fits in with God's plan. For over ten years, I have served in various marketing positions for HealthEast, a system of hospitals and health-related services. Our organization's mission is closely tied to Christ's healing ministry. With hospital names like St. John's, St. Joseph's, and Bethesda (named after the healing pool in John 5:2), one would be hard-pressed to forget our religious ties. Yet health care is still a business (a big one at that) and marketing would seem to be as far removed from that healing ministry as one could get. Most hospitals did not have marketing departments until census levels sharply declined in the 1980s, so many in the field view them as a necessary evil. Some administrators feel hospitals should concentrate more time on healing people and less on "hawking their wares."

In seeking spiritual meaning in my work, I looked at how my job of marketing helped our firm serve its customers. A health care company's main purpose is to help people recover from illness and reach their maximum potential level of health. My job, in marketing, is to identify unmet or undermet health needs in the community through market research, then help develop or change services to meet those needs, and finally inform the community of our ability to meet those needs. Helping identify and meet community health needs seems to me to be a very legitimate and rewarding ministry. The efforts of my department have led to the development of unique services needed by the community, improved customer access to health services, and greater awareness of resources available to keep people healthier.

Health care may be a little easier tie-in to ministry because of its comparison to the acts of healing in the Bible. Yet even a corner service station can play a role in God's ministry. I remember taking frequent drives to a friend's house and wondering about the surprising lack of gas stations. This long, well-traveled highway ran through a large, prosperous residential area which had many retailers. *If someone would put a station on this road,* I thought, *people living here could save the time and fuel they now spend hunting for a distant gas station.* If the station had service bays to work on cars and did quality work, it could ease some of the frustration and inconvenience that goes along with a malfunctioning car. Having such a service within walking distance would be extremely important to many one-vehicle families. By making life more convenient for people in the neighborhood, that little station might contribute to the growth of the community, as well as provide jobs. If those running

> **Any good work done for the glory of God is religious work.**

the station are committed Christians and seek to honor God in their business, they could have a real, thriving ministry on that corner. (By the way, someone did eventually put a big gas station on that highway, and it looks as if business is booming.)

As I began to see how work in industry could serve God, it broke down the limiting walls of my old view of ministry. When I used to think about serving in the body of Christ, I didn't look much beyond my local church congregation. I now see how God's ministry encompasses all areas of a person's life. This has opened my eyes to many new avenues of service to God.

We need to see that ministry is not just activities done by churches and missionaries. Any good work done for the glory of God is religious work. It only becomes secular when we leave God out of it. According to A.W. Tozer, our motives and attitudes toward work mean everything.

It is not what a man does that determines whether his work is sacred or secular, it is *why* he does it. The motive is everything. Let a man sanctify the Lord God in his heart and he can thereafter do no common act. All he does is good and acceptable to God through Jesus Christ. For such a man, living itself will be sacramental and the whole world a sanctuary. His entire life will be a priestly ministration. As he performs his never so simple task he will hear the voice of the seraphim saying, "Holy, Holy, Holy, is the Lord of hosts: the whole earth is full of his glory."[1]

Think about It

❏ Do you view your own work as a curse, a ministry, or something in-between? Why?

❏ Write down three tasks you will tackle during your next work day. Would you normally consider these to be sacred or secular activities? What changes do you need to make in order to change any secular tasks into sacred?

Notes

1. A.W. Tozer, *The Pursuit of God* (Harrisburg, Pa.: Christian Publications, Inc., 1948), 127-128.

3

Your Work Is God's Business

I n the last chapter, we built the case for expanding our concept of ministry to include all of our life—including our work. At this point some of you are probably thinking, *Now what? What does ministry in the work world amount to anyhow? Does God provide us with some concrete answers or are we just supposed to wing it?*

The easiest thing to do would be wing it. A few years ago, if someone had asked me what it means to be a Christian in the marketplace, I would have struggled to come up with much in the way of specifics. I might have stammered out scattered suggestions like not laughing at dirty jokes, not stealing from my employer, and being ready to share my faith with those around me. I've been in discussions with other Christians on this question, and in most cases, their answers were as general as mine.

After my search of the Bible, mentioned in chapter 1, I realized that God is very concerned about work activities. He designed a world where those activities are necessary, and He provided specific guidance for them in hundreds of separate Bible references.

In the next two chapters, we'll develop a biblical perspective of work, seeing how our work relates to God and His work. We'll also see why our work efforts have spiritual significance and value. This discussion will then provide the framework for building specific components of our work ministry. I will introduce these later in the book.

God Cares about the Details of Work

Many people in our world today view God (if they even believe He exists) as a distant observer in our lives. He may have had a hand in getting the merry-go-round of life started (depending on one's position in the evolution/creation debate), but now He stands on the sidelines like a concerned parent, watching His children ride the painted ponies, offering a smile and an encouraging word as they ride up and down.

Fortunately, that is not the kind of God portrayed in the Bible. Ours is an involved God. His involvement is not limited to traditionally spiritual matters such as people being saved, but includes practical daily tasks such as providing food, clothing, and shelter for our families. The whole world is God's, and He is an owner who pays great attention to details.

Let's look at three roles or functions God serves that relate to our work: God as mentor, God as boss, and God as coworker.

God As Mentor

A mentor serves as a trusted counselor or guide, someone more knowledgeable in the field who can show the newcomer the ropes. Many business experts link having a mentor with a successful career.

Mentor relationships can vary considerably in terms of their length and the type of guidance they offer. My first mentor was in college. I met with Dave Rowe from Campus Ambassadors nearly every week to talk and study the Bible. It was a discipling process that was brief, occasionally intense, and set the stage for future spiritual growth.

In the business world, I've been fortunate to learn from many experienced people. For example, I met Clay Atkinson while he was looking to do some marketing consulting with my employer. He has many years of experience with some of the top corporations in the country. Our relationship has been ongoing and extremely casual. We get together periodically to discuss our marketing projects. I find it helpful to run my strategies and ideas by someone who can raise questions and issues I had not considered.

You've probably been on one end or another of a mentor relationship at some point in your life. Usually, we also realize that these relationships have limits. Eventually, the person being mentored will possess enough knowledge to carry on alone or will seek others who have additional knowledge in additional areas.

While human mentors may be limited and even flawed, we have access to a perfect mentor: God. The Old Testament is filled with accounts of God's work. The first two chapters of Genesis show God as a very hardworking Creator. In addition to big tasks like making the heavens and the earth, God was also involved in the detail work of forming man from the dust of the ground (Gen. 2:7), planting a garden in Eden (Gen. 2:8), and making woman from the rib of Adam (Gen. 2:21-22). Every time I take a walk in the woods or watch a panoramic sunset I marvel at what God has created.

Although God rested on the seventh day, He didn't go into retirement after Creation. The Psalms frequently refer to the ongoing work of God. Psalm 121 repeatedly proclaims that God "watches over" us continually, helping us and keeping us from harm. Psalm 104 praises God for His many works, noting that all creation looks to Him who ensures they are "satisfied with good things." In fact, virtually every book in the Old Testament shows God at work with the people of Israel, protecting them, instructing them, inspiring them, and punishing them.

Why does God do His work with such fanfare and high visibility? He could easily have kept it hidden from us, modestly going about His job without recognition or honor. If a fellow executive maintained God's kind of profile, we might accuse him or her of having a swelled ego. Not God. He has no need to boast. Instead, He shows us His work as a model to strive toward.

A good example of modeling proper behavior for us occurs in the Creation account in Genesis. We all know that on the seventh day God rested. Did our all-powerful God need to rest? Of course not! As any good mentor would do, God was showing us the proper way to approach work. God explains this in the Fourth Commandment found in Exodus 20:8-11:

> Remember the Sabbath day by keeping it holy. Six days you shall labor and do all your work, but the seventh day is a Sabbath to the LORD your God. On it you shall not do any work, neither you, nor your son or daughter, nor your manservant or maidservant, nor your animals, nor the alien with-

in your gates. For in six days the Lord made the heavens and the earth, the sea, and all that is in them, but He rested on the seventh day. Therefore the LORD blessed the Sabbath day and made it holy.

The next time you read the Bible, pay close attention to the way God conducts His affairs. According to Wheaton College (Illinois) professor Leland Ryken, we can learn volumes from closely examining how God works:

> The work of God, even though it is unique, remains a model for human work. It affirms that work is good and Godlike in principle. The work of God is creative, orderly, and constructive. It is universal. It benefits people and other creatures. It declares the very nature of God and bears his imprint or signature. Human work can do no better than emulate God's work.[1]

All legitimate work has spiritual value because work itself is a godly activity. That is a concept that has been long lost in our culture, with its secular/sacred distinctions which restrict our spiritual life to an hour or two on Sundays.

For me, it is easiest to see my labor emulating God's work when I discover an enjoyable new task or skill. I always planned to teach someday but, being an introvert, I didn't try it until my late twenties. In my nervous preparations, I leaned heavily on God, who showed me all the gifts He had already given me for the task. When I taught, I felt God's creativity at work within me, and I saw the effects of that on my students. Even if the subject matter is not religious, teaching remains for me one of the most spiritual tasks I perform.

> **All legitimate work has spiritual value because work itself is a godly activity.**

Jesus: A Model Worker

In the New Testament, God provides us with another perfect mentor: His Son. Jesus, being both fully man and fully God, bridged the gap that sin created between God and man. He also helps us see the relationship of our work to the work of God.

One thing that stands out in the work life of Jesus is the amount of time He spent doing what we call common, everyday work. Christ was a carpenter until the age of thirty, spending less than 10 percent of His life in formal ministry.

Why did He wait so long? Could He have left home at age eighteen and started His formal ministry? Probably. He was God, after all. The Bible only has one reference to the life of Jesus between the ages of twelve and thirty—found in Luke 2:52. After His boyhood experience in the temple, Jesus returned to Nazareth and "grew in wisdom and stature." Theologians speculate that this was a time of preparation for the great tasks that would lie ahead. What did He do to prepare Himself? All the evidence suggests that He lived similarly to those around Him: He worked, played, enjoyed life, worshiped, and studied the Scriptures.

This fact hits me hard when I try to downplay the work I do every day, particularly when I compare it to those involved in formal ministry. Our struggles in the work world cannot be seen as insignificant since Christ Himself spent most of His adult life engaged in those same activities. How can we call something God does secular or non-spiritual? We can't. Christ glorified work by devoting the bulk of His life to that activity.

Jesus also provides a model of how we are to relate our work to God the Father. In John 4:34, He states that His purpose is "to do the will of Him who sent me and to finish His work." Most of us give comparatively little thought to God's will for our lives. Nearly every day I catch myself making business decisions and setting work priorities without any thought about God and His priorities. Christ always kept tuned in to the will of His Father and submitted to it.

Not only does Jesus serve as a mentor for us, but He also illustrates a mentor relationship by describing how He relates to His Father. In John 5:17, Jesus defends His action of healing on the Sabbath by saying, "My Father is always at His work to this very day, and I, too, am working." God was His model and guide for His work. He goes on to explain further in verse 19:

Jesus gave them this answer: "I tell you the truth, the Son can do nothing by Himself; He can do only what He sees His

Father doing, because whatever the Father does the Son also does."

How can we have this mentor relationship? Studying the Scriptures and prayer can help us transform our work and provide insight into key business decisions. Larry Burkett, author and founder of Christian Financial Concepts, noted that Exodus 18 helped him make a critical decision affecting the future direction of his financial and business advisory ministry. In this chapter, Jethro visited Moses and noticed that his son-in-law spent all day judging disputes among the Israelites. People often waited hours or even days to see him. Jethro told Moses not to shoulder all the burden himself, but to delegate power to others so he would only need to handle the most difficult cases.

"And that's what I have done in this ministry," Burkett recalled. "I've gone and found myself the best administrator possible...and then let him run the organization." According to Burkett, learning the principle of delegation from the Bible is "paying off," allowing him to concentrate on the tasks he does best. [2]

God is the source of all true wisdom. If we are to choose a mentor for our lives, what better choice could we make than to follow our all-powerful and all-knowing God? The Bible paints a very clear picture of how He works, providing ample opportunities to apply His example to our own work.

> **If we are to choose a mentor for our lives, what better choice could we make than to follow our all-powerful and all-knowing God?**

God As Boss

Sometimes, in the work world, our primary mentor also happens to be our boss. Whether the two figures are the same person or not, the two roles vary considerably. While the mentor serves as our role model, the boss is our authority figure—the one who holds us responsible for our actions on the job. As Christians, no matter what kind of work we do, God needs to be our boss.

Now seeing God as your boss may or may not be considered a good thing, depending on your past experiences with your earthly bosses. The people you reported to over the years may have often asked the impossible, found nothing good in the work you did, and made you feel genuinely inadequate and inferior. Not God. He's always concerned about our welfare and is always willing to lighten our burdens when we feel overwhelmed.

The word *boss* is really a bit limited when used to describe God because His responsibility is so vast compared to human executives. Our Lord is the world's chief executive officer, chairman of the board, and sole stockholder all in one. Psalm 24:1-2 describes His domain: "The earth is the Lord's, and everything in it, the world, and all who live in it; for He founded it upon the seas and established it upon the waters."

On earth, then, none of us can ever say we are truly the boss. Even the fiercely independent entrepreneur, who may have built his or her business "from the ground up," has reason to concede superiority to the one who made the ground and everything else that forms the basis of the world economy. Most Christian entrepreneurs I have met are quick to point out that their business belongs to God.

Just as supervisors provide work tasks and instructions to those they manage, God also gives mankind a job to do. In Genesis 1:28, God tells man to "subdue" the earth and rule over it. He gave us an entire world to work with and enjoy. Psalm 8:5-8 conveys some of the wonder of this act of delegation and describes the high honor man has received from God:

> You made him a little lower than the heavenly beings and
> crowned him with glory and honor.
> You made him ruler over the works
> of your hands; you put everything
> under his feet: all flocks and herds,
> and the beasts of the field, the birds
> of the air, and the fish of the sea,
> all that swim the paths of the seas.

> **God meant for our work in this world to be a high honor.**

Our work was never intended to be drudgery or punishment. God meant for our work in this world to be a high honor.

Could our omnipotent God have run the earth better Himself?

Certainly! Could He have grown more food, created more prosperity, and better preserved the environment if He had just bypassed those bumbling humans and performed all the work Himself? Yes, I think the world's Creator could handle that.

Instead, He chose to exalt and honor us by delegating part of His divine activities, giving us a chance to grow and fail, a chance to imitate the God in whose image we were created. We participate in the godly task of subduing and ruling the earth when we do our jobs well, develop a new product or service, open a new store, or even when we plant the family vegetable garden. The fact that we are sinful and imperfect in carrying out our calling does not strip our work of its spiritual significance.

What are the implications of seeing God as our boss?

First, we need to conduct our business in a way that honors God and furthers His work on earth.

Second, as Christians, we should now have better motivation to work "with all your heart," as commanded in Colossians 3:23, because now we report to our Lord and Savior, not just to the guy who told you that you wouldn't be getting a raise this coming year. Having this new boss, however, does not give us the freedom to ignore any human bosses we currently have—the New Testament is filled with numerous commands for Christian slaves to obey their earthly masters. Those passages addressed to slaves also assure us that we have a God who will reward our good work (Eph. 6:8; Col. 3:24) and, unlike any other master, He shows no favoritism among those who work for Him (Eph. 6:9).

Finally, unlike some earthly supervisors, we can confide in our God, sharing all our struggles and ideas without the threat of it appearing on our next performance review. Several Christians in my classes have mentioned that, although they work for jerks on the job, knowing they ultimately report to a caring God makes it easier to deal with the "middleman."

God As Coworker

Have you ever had a supervisor who simply doled out projects with no explanation of what was expected and no offer of assistance should you have difficulties? In fact, the only real communication you received from such a person was when you "messed up."

Fortunately for us, God does not treat His workers that way. Our Lord is a boss who works in the trenches with His people. God is not only available to labor with us and help us but, without His involvement, our work is useless. Those are pretty strong words, but the Bible is very clear about the futility of work apart from God. Psalm 127:1-2 says that work done without the help and guidance of the Lord is in vain:

> Unless the LORD builds the house, its builders labor in vain. Unless the LORD watches over the city, the watchmen stand guard in vain. In vain you rise early and stay up late, toiling for food to eat—for He grants sleep to those He loves.

Those who run on the business fast track without God are essentially running a race that has neither a finish line nor prizes.

In Ecclesiastes, Solomon talks repeatedly about the vanity or meaninglessness of life and work apart from God. Part of the meaninglessness of laboring independently of God is that we may be struggling to do something that He does not want done. Ecclesiastes 7:13 tells us: "Consider what God has done: Who can straighten what he has made crooked?" Nothing is more futile than trying to work against God.

I get a clear illustration of working with or against God every summer at our lake property. Every time we mow and trim grass to make the place more "civilized," it only takes a couple weeks of absence to undo our efforts. On the other hand, I feel as if I'm working with God when I plant trees to bring back the woods cleared by previous owners. The God-given processes of nature, combined with my efforts, have helped restore some of the landscape in a few short years.

In addition to avoiding futility, working with God is our only chance for satisfaction and enjoyment. Ecclesiastes 2:24-25 states that satisfaction with work is "from the hand of God," noting that enjoyment is impossible to find without God.

Even Jesus, the Son of God, admitted in John 5:19 that He could do nothing by Himself. He also provides a vivid illustration of our dependency upon God and Himself in John 15:1-8. Christ is described as the vine, we are the branches, and God is the gardener. The vine provides what is needed for the branches to bear fruit because branches, cut off from the vine, "can do nothing." God prunes the branches which, as any of you with gardening experience undoubtedly know, increases the yield. For us to be fruitful in any part of our life and ministry, we need to maintain a strong relationship with Jesus Christ.

The Bible is packed with examples of God working with His people to accomplish great things. My favorite story is that of Nehemiah and the rebuilding of the wall of Jerusalem. This was a very tangible problem, not unlike those we face at work. After the exile of the Jews, the city of Jerusalem and the wall that surrounded it were in ruins. The times were not good for God's chosen people.

> **For us to be fruitful in any part of our life and ministry, we need to maintain a strong relationship with Jesus Christ.**

Nehemiah shows us how to successfully work with God. After many days of prayer, God enabled him to go to Jerusalem to begin construction. Despite immense and potentially violent opposition to the project, Nehemiah and the Jewish remnant began the project, confident that "the God of Heaven will give us success." At every obstacle and challenge, the group turned to God in prayer, and He sustained their effort.

Nehemiah also remained faithful to God's Word. When he learned that Jews were lending money to pay the king's tax and grain for food to other Jews at excessive interest, Nehemiah rebuked them for disobeying God's command against usury and made them stop the practice. In Nehemiah 6:15-16, the story ends with a wall that had been completed in just fifty-two days under difficult circumstances. Those nations and people who had opposed the construction "lost their self-confidence because they realized that this work had been done with the help of our God."

As with Nehemiah, our Lord can be a powerful coworker in our work projects, large and small. Spending time in His Word and in prayer are the keys. Several businessmen at a weekly Bible study I attend have said that praying while driving into work has made a big difference in how they approach their job activities. Everyday work problems don't seem to bother them as much and their tasks seem to take on greater spiritual significance. They don't leave their prayers at the front door, either. Throughout the day, these men also fire off brief prayers of gratitude when things go well, or they ask for God's assistance when faced with a crisis.

In looking through the Bible, it becomes apparent that we do not have to struggle through our business activities alone. We have a God who cares about our work because He is a worker as well. Through His roles as mentor, boss, and coworker, God provides all the help and guidance we need to conduct our business in a way that honors Him and fulfills His will for the world. Just as our human mentor/boss/coworker relationships benefit when we spend time trying to develop them, strengthening our relationship with God through prayer and Bible reading is essential to making our business work a ministry.

Think about It

❑ If God is your ultimate boss, which of your current projects do you think He would consider most important? Is there a project you haven't gotten around to yet that you think God would value greatly?

❑ Next time you notice God's work, either through His creation or answered prayer, ask yourself: "What lesson can I learn from witnessing God's work that I can apply to my day-to-day activities?

Notes

1. Leland Ryken, *Work & Leisure in Christian Perspective* (Portland: Multnomah Press, 1987), 122.
2. Larry Burkett, "Delegate and Let God Use Others!" *Spiritual Fitness in Business 2*, No. 4 (April 1984): 4.

4

The Spiritual Benefits of
Working in Business

....

ave you ever hired someone whom you thought was the
perfect candidate for the job—good work experience with
all the right companies, sound academic background, glowing recommendations—only to discover the person to be surprisingly ineffective when it came to performing his job duties? Based on credentials, you expected a top performer, not someone just trying to muddle through the day. How disappointing it is when someone who has all the personal tools necessary to do outstanding work flounders.

Sometimes I feel like that employee. Sometimes I also wonder if God doesn't feel like that disappointed boss. When I reflect on what God has provided for working believers, as we discussed in the last chapter, I feel as if my progress to date has been most inadequate. With God as my mentor, boss, and coworker, how could I be anything but an awe-inspiring sight on the job?

Many days, however, I feel as if I am blending into the woodwork instead of standing out. At times of high stress, I often catch myself grumbling and complaining at least as much as other employees. And I sometimes find myself going through the motions instead of working with great enthusiasm and energy.

Why does this happen to us? If work is indeed something God provided for our benefit, then why is it so grueling and frustrating sometimes? God's answer to those questions is simply this: the curse.

When I was first attempting to live out my faith at work, I halfway felt that work was the curse God had placed on humanity after the fall of Adam. All the struggles and conflicts on the job fit neatly into such a theory. My assignment was to simply endure this punishment until retirement—preferably a very early retirement brought about by launching an outlandishly successful business or by winning a major mail-order sweepstakes. Then I could live the Eden-like life of leisure I was meant to live, forever free of the curse of work.

My grandiose plans were foiled when I looked closely at the first few chapters of Genesis. God put Adam in the Garden of Eden "to work it and take care of it" (Gen. 2:15), *before* Adam sinned and brought about the curse. God, a worker, created man in His image and gave him work to do in the world He created.

Many other ancient religions also have creation accounts that describe man as being created to work—but merely as slaves of the gods. Biblical scholars point to the Genesis account as a dramatic departure from the myths and beliefs of the cultures surrounding the Jews.

> In fact the biblical story actually contradicts the notion of humans as slaves and of work as the gods' chores. Note the order of the created things: the man, then the garden. The man was not made to work the garden of God, as in other creation stories. Rather the garden was made by God as a habitable place for the man. Thus the garden is man's, and his work in tilling and preserving the garden is intended for his own benefit. Work is viewed here as part of God's creation and is to be undertaken in the shalom-like relationship between God and his human creatures. This work—provided as one of God's blessings, along with food to eat, beauty to behold, and companionship to enjoy—is for human welfare in the world which God worked so hard to create.[1]

Work, then, was never intended to be a burden, a curse, or a punishment. Sin changed that. Fallen man's entire relationship to God was severely affected by sin. Sin created a gap, a separation from God that would require a true Savior to close it.

Since man's relationship to God was altered because of sin, it is only natural that man's major activity—work—also changed. It is impossible for God to act as man's mentor, boss, and coworker when we are separated from Him because of our sin. For a pure God can have nothing to do with sin.

With the fall of Adam and Eve, sin entered the world and its work. Created as inherently good, work was corrupted by the effects of sin, making it worshiped by workaholics, scorned by the lazy, and abused by the greedy. Working with others became more difficult, whether the relationship was master and slave, boss and employee, seller and buyer, or coworkers. Today's marketplace, too often built upon a foundation of greed and ambition, can blame much of its malfunctioning and cruelty on sin and its effects.

> **Created as inherently good, work was corrupted by the effects of sin, making it worshiped by workaholics, scorned by the lazy, and abused by the greedy.**

As a result of sin, work in the garden became labor in the fields. I find it very interesting that our English language uses the same word, *labor*, to describe both the process of work and childbearing. (The word is also the same in Latin.) It would not surprise me if the application of the curse to those two activities in Genesis 3:16-17 had a lot to do with the development of the term *labor*. In fact, the ancient Hebrew manuscripts use derivatives of the same word to describe the pain, toil, and suffering of both childbirth and work. Both activities have become a pain because of the curse, one arduous and long-suffering, another short-term but very acute.

Is that all there is, then? Is work supposed to be good but instead is a pain, so just make the best of it? For a while, this was my complete view of work. It is not a very hopeful picture, particularly when you contrast it with the promise of redemption and salvation through Jesus Christ.

To regain a hopeful attitude toward work, I had to understand that accepting Christ as my Savior transforms (or at least should transform) my entire life. Becoming a Christian not only affects my after-life destination but should also impact my family life, church life, and even my work life. According to Leland Ryken, although work has become cursed, Christ offers a solution:

...the whole pattern of Christian theology is to offer a solution to the problems occasioned by sin. Work can be redeemed, even in a fallen world. Anything that helps us to overcome the effects of sin on work is part of this redemption. Work itself retains some of the quality of a curse, but the attitude of the worker can transform it.[2]

Christ brings hope to the marketplace because He offers to restore us to a right relationship to God—a prerequisite to working the way God intended for us. Once we have that right relationship, we can let God help us transform our work life. That transformation takes place gradually through daily prayer, submission to God's will, and developing a godly attitude toward work.

In my own case, I pray every day on my drive to the office. I ask for God to be with me that day, commit all my work to Him, and I ask for guidance and wisdom and for opportunities to be a witness for Him whether in word or deed. Starting work with prayer and submission gives me a better attitude. I notice the difference on days when I forget to start with prayer.

Is my work transformation complete and the curse a thing of the past? No. I'm afraid I have a long journey ahead of me. Although I still have a mix of both good days and ugly ones, I have seen gradual improvement in the way I approach my work and the amount of joy and fulfillment it brings me.

Six Spiritual Benefits of Work

So do those of us caught in the daily grind just keep praying and hoping for the curse to go away? Fortunately, God offers a little more hope for us than that. He provides a better answer than my parents did to the question of why we should work: "Because we said so." Although often effective in motivating me, these words would hardly be considered inspirational. Despite the lingering effects of the curse, God has designed work in a way that benefits us spiritually.

Benefit #1: Work provides for our family's needs. At first glance, this benefit does not appear to have a spiritual component. After all, we work, we get paid, we get by. To God, however, the act of providing for one's family is very important indeed. Paul, in his letters to the early church, frequently exhorts believers to continue to be productive and provide for their families. In 1 Timothy 5:8, Paul states that whoever does not provide for his family and relatives "has denied the faith and is worse than an unbeliever."

To say someone has denied the faith is awfully strong language. That is how important work is to God. In Paul's day, many new believers spent all their time concerned with church and other "spiritual" matters, ignoring their earthly responsibilities. God's world, however, is set up so those who want to have food, clothing, and shelter for themselves and their families can obtain it through honest labor. Living by the fruit of one's labor is better for us, according to God, than living off the fruit of others through hand-outs or exploitation.

Although our imperfect world economy often creates situations where jobs are difficult to find for some people, God has created a system that allows us to provide—sometimes quite amply—for our families. Proverbs 14:23 reminds us that "all hard work brings a profit, but mere talk leads only to poverty." This proverb may not always run true in the short-run. We all know of businesses that failed despite the hard work of their owners. Over the long haul, however, I cannot think of a single hardworking person I have met who has not been able to scrape together at least a modest living. Psalm 128:1-2 states that one of the blessings of fearing God and following His instruction is to "eat the fruit of your labor." What a basic but crucial benefit to working for God!

Those of you with employees should feel responsibility for providing for their families as well, particularly in an era when layoffs are so commonly accepted by management. In 1983, Garman Kimmell of Kimray, Inc. was forced to lay off 85 employees to avoid going bankrupt. Eliminating jobs that supported so many families hurt Kimmell deeply. He vowed to set aside a portion of company earnings when the economy recovered, so they would be ready for the next "rainy day."

Three years later, the oil industry that Kimray supplies took another downturn. Kimmell cut costs again, but this time he did not lay off a single employee. Instead of collecting unemployment, workers researched new machinery and techniques, went through job cross-training and product training, and were even paid to volunteer for all kinds of civic projects. Besides providing for employee families, Kimmell's strong witness gained widespread attention.[3]

Benefit #2: Work provides a means for meeting many of our own needs. Besides putting food on the family table, work can meet many other personal needs as well. God did not intend for work to be pure drudgery. Ecclesiastes 5:18 declares that it is "good and proper" to find satisfaction in our "toilsome" labor. Even with the effects of the curse and sin in the workplace, we can still feel a sense of accomplishment and satisfaction in a job well done. Just as God looked back on His Creation work and saw that it was "good," we need to capture some of that same spirit of accomplishment at the end of our own workday.

Now some jobs out there are menial, meaningless, and even immoral. For example, it would be impossible for someone running a pornography shop to feel the same sense of spiritual accomplishment as someone involved in the business of bringing food to the tables of families. I believe, however, that we are all created to perform certain work activities and that, using our God-given abilities, we can enjoy an immense sense of satisfaction. (We will discuss this more in chapter 5.) My greatest career joy comes when I am involved in activities related to my interests and abilities which, in my case, include marketing, teaching, and writing.

In our society, we have given work such a bad name that the mere thought of making it enjoyable seems like a fantasy. I remember a friend of mine in graduate school who was both bewildered and amused that I would be interested in finding rewarding work, instead of simply accepting the highest-paying job offer I could get. She grew up in a neighborhood where most people worked on the assembly line and lived for the weekend. True enjoyment could only come after punching out at the end of a shift. Career fulfillment, to her, was a foreign concept.

Finding joy in work seems even more foreign to today's youth. A few years ago, I wrote an article for a Christian youth publication. My original title was "Doing What You Love for a Living" yet, after reviewing it with her teen advisory board, the editor changed the title to "Careers You Could Love." Most of the teens could not buy into the concept that work could be fun.

God teaches that work can not only be enjoyable, but that a job well done can also better us in more tangible ways. Take Proverbs 22:29 for instance: "Do you see a man skilled in his work? He will serve before kings; he will not serve before obscure men." The Bible is loaded with examples of people rewarded for their skillful work: Joseph, David, Daniel, and Jeroboam (whom King Solomon promoted when he saw how well he did his work).

> **In our society, we have given work such a bad name that the mere thought of making it enjoyable seems like a fantasy.**

In short, God has given work value, not just in the money it provides, but also in the sense of accomplishment and fulfillment that comes from a job well done.

Benefit #3: Work provides a substantial way for us to serve others. In Matthew 20:26-28, Christ commands us to live a life of service to others:

> Whoever wants to become great among you must be your servant, and whoever wants to be first must be your slave—just as the Son of Man did not come to be served, but to serve, and to give His life as a ransom for many.

Living a life of Christian service is not limited to activities like church work and volunteering at a nursing home. In the world of work, Christians can see their work in a more spiritual way: as service to mankind.

We can look at how our work serves others in two ways: how it fits into God's big picture of providing for our needs, and how we are able to serve those we have contact with as workers.

Now God's big picture of service is big indeed. God uses the people working in our immensely complicated economic systems to meet the needs of His people. When we thank God for our daily bread, we need to realize that God did not simply toss the food down from heaven. (Moses and the Israelites in Exodus were the only ones to experience that.) God uses people to provide our food—the seed dealer, farmer, farm equipment dealer, food processor, wholesaler, trucker, and grocer, to name a few.

The concept that God uses us to provide for the wide-ranging needs of others provides tremendous justification for business activity. A basic marketing and entrepreneurial principle is to find a market with a need and fill it. Sometimes that need is physical or material. Sometimes it is social or even spiritual. Whatever the case, when we meet any legitimate human need, we improve the quality of life for others.

Even the most commonplace of products or services can help others far more than their creators could ever imagine. The people who make the often-maligned frozen dinner have no idea how much they helped out my father. My mother developed Alzheimer's disease before the age of 60, forcing my hardworking executive father into becoming the family cook (a task he was ill-equipped to perform). As her disease progressed, my mother felt increasingly uncomfortable going out for dinner, and her taste buds were far too finicky to tolerate most home-delivered meals. Fortunately for my father, frozen foods have come a long way from the tasteless "TV dinners" I grew up with. Today's selections often taste almost home-made, offer immensely greater variety, and can be highly nutritious. As a result, my father was able to quickly prepare a quality meal (that my mother would eat) at the end of a long day at the office. If any of you reading this have ever been involved in getting these dinners into the grocer's freezer case, please know that you have served one family well. Thanks!

On a macro level, service to others can be even more basic. If your efforts have helped your business expand and hire more people, then you have provided the means for more men, women, and teenagers to make a living. In today's economy, anyone who can create jobs is providing a great service to humanity. Imagine hearing the prayers of a once-unemployed father or mother—thanking God for providing a job to feed and clothe their children—knowing that God had used your efforts and your company to answer that cry for help.

We also need to remember the "little" picture, however, taking advantage of all the opportunities to serve those we come in contact with at work: coworkers, customers, suppliers, bosses, and subordinates. The service we give them can take a wide variety of forms. We can serve others partly through commendable job performance, by meeting their needs as workers or customers. We can also serve others by performing our role as Christ's ambassador to people with struggles, concerns, and hurts. (That covers about everyone we meet each day.)

Our approach to serving others is nicely outlined in Philippians 2:4-7:

> Each of you should look not only to your own interests, but also to the interests of others. Your attitude should be the same as that of Christ Jesus: Who, being in very nature God, did not consider equality with God something to be grasped, but made Himself nothing, taking the very nature of a servant, being made in human likeness.

Applying this passage to work goes against the "old school" principle of only looking out for number one. I use the term *old* because it would be hard to find any "nice guys finish last" management experts around today. Bob Swiggett of Kollmorgen —one of the top executives from "excellent" companies often quoted by management expert Tom Peters—put it this way:

> The role of the leader is a servant's role. It's supporting his people, running interference for them. It's coming out with an atmosphere of understanding and trust—and love. You want people to feel they have complete control over their destiny at every level. Tyranny is not tolerated here. People who want to manage in the traditional sense are cast off by their peers like dandruff.... We preach trust and the golden rule.[4]

In my own experience, most successful executives I have met have been more concerned with the needs of people—their employees and their customers—than with how they can claw their way up the next rung of the ladder of success. When my father reflected on his successful career at G & K Services, he did not dwell on the positions he held or the money he made. He felt his crowning achievement was the number of executives he had hired, trained, and guided who had developed into outstanding managers and risen to high posts in the organization. My father spent many hours with these managers to help them realize their full potential in their work. His subordinates benefited from this service, the company had a supply of highly trained managers to help it expand, and my father increased his value to the organization.

Providing service to others, then, whether through outstanding, caring performance of our job duties or providing a patient ear or word of encouragement, is an outstanding spiritual benefit to work. I think all people have within themselves a desire to make a difference, to see that their efforts matter. Realizing how our work serves others can provide meaning to nearly any work, according to Ryken:

> To view work as a form of service to humanity redeems almost any task that is in itself unrewarding. It is the great balancing factor to that work which carries its own reward and which we find inherently satisfying. Much of the work we do does not rise to that ideal.... To view ourselves as serving others can give such work a moral purpose and a reason to be satisfied in doing it. If at any point in our lives we are involved in work we cannot defend as being a genuine service to others, we should look for other work.[5]

Benefit #4: Work provides financially so we can share with others. In Ephesians 4:28, Paul exhorts the idle to steal no longer but to instead perform useful work so that they "may have something to share with those in need." Besides providing us with income to support ourselves and our families, God blesses our work with rewards that enable us to share generously with others.

Generosity with money is a tough topic that is far too complex to be covered here in any depth. My own view on generosity is this: if we all share our money as freely as we share our opinions, then there would be no needy or hungry people in the world. It is pretty easy to tell people what we think about something. Some of us also share our faith quite freely (although I still find I am more selective about sharing my testimony than about sharing my political views). Opening our pocketbooks, however, often requires an entirely different level of commitment.

Although all people need to hear the message concerning Jesus Christ, sometimes they need even more to see that message in action. The unemployed worker may need help with groceries for a time. The person with inadequate health insurance may need some help with medical bills after an extended illness and hospital stay. A homeless person living on the downtown streets may need a few dollars for his or her next meal. I haven't yet mentioned church giving, supporting mission work, and feeding the starving in Africa.

Sometimes generosity is more involved than simply writing out a check. A friend of mine, who was a cement contractor, often donated his time and materials to do cement work and other projects at a Christian camp. The time spent there could have been profitably devoted to moneymaking projects.

In this world, God has provided numerous opportunities for us to give to others. He also assures us that, if we give generously, He will make sure that our own needs are still met. Proverbs 3:9-10 says to "honor the LORD with your wealth, with the firstfruits of all your crops; then your barns will be filled to overflowing, and your vats will brim over with new wine."

This passage does not mean God will make you rich if you write a big check to your favorite charity. Instead, God tells us we need to reserve a portion of our earnings for Him all the time, not just when we have some extra cash left over at the end of the week. When we faithfully turn our money over to Him, God will supply the means for that giving to continue. In Psalm 37:25-26, King David reflected on the viability of those who are generous and righteous:

> I was young and now I am old, yet I have never seen the righteous forsaken or their children begging bread. They are always generous and lend freely; their children will be blessed.

I am still learning the lesson of God honoring faithful giving. When I reduced my working hours at HealthEast to allow time for other work, my salary took a 40 percent nosedive. Kathy and I decided we would not reduce our church and other contributions, because that was the minimum amount we felt we ought to be giving. In the first two years of that reduced income, our giving actually increased and, for the first time in our marriage, we actually started putting money aside for savings and investments. God injected us with a modest dose of frugality, which helped us become more generous and less wasteful with our money.

Those striving to be increasingly generous face extremely difficult obstacles in our society, where materialism has run amok for far too long. Giving 10 percent of one's earnings was the rule in the Israel of the Old Testament, yet today people who give that much are uncommon and are considered outstanding financial stewards. Materialism and the love of money are a disease that paralyzes our ability to give, because it creates desires that are never satisfied. Ecclesiastes 5:10 states, "Whoever loves money never has money enough; whoever loves wealth is never satisfied with his income." How true.

> **Just as God's love should overflow from our hearts to others, so should the fruit of our labor flow fro m our pocketbooks to meet the needs around us.**

In spite of our ongoing battle with the love of money, our income from work is still a spiritual benefit because it gives us the ability to be generous. Just as God's love should overflow from our hearts to others, so should the fruit of our labor flow from our pocketbooks to meet the needs around us.

Benefit #5: Work provides both an opportunity and a means for witnessing to others. Since I devote an entire chapter to witnessing at the end of this book, I will spend only a few lines talking about it here. The key point is that work is both a setting for sharing the Gospel *and* a means for witnessing to others.

If you labor in a typical employment setting, you can understand what a potential mission field exists in the workplace. For many Christians who grew up in Christian families and had most of their social activities center around church, the workplace may be the only mission field available to them. In most cases, our employment causes us to interact with large numbers of people, providing opportunities to demonstrate our faith with our actions and to share our faith with our words.

When he sells financial services, Randy Larson finds that his work brings him into substantial contact with a variety of people. He says he can get to know a lot about someone by listening to him discuss his finances. Sometimes, he realizes, financial services are not what the person needs right now. "When I come across someone who is hurting spiritually, I'll drop the business discussion and share the Gospel instead."

If a church wishes to uncover evangelistic outreach opportunities, I encourage them to poll their congregation regarding places of employment and the number of people working at each site. Even a church with less than 100 members might still have footholds in dozens of organizations employing hundreds, perhaps thousands, of people. What potential!

Our jobs do not simply have spiritual significance by bringing us into contact with non-Christians so we can hand out tracts and lead others to Christ. The work itself is a witness, good or bad, depending on its quality. Being skilled, competent, hardworking, and cooperative will have a great impact on our ability to form work relationships that will contain enough mutual respect for an effective verbal witness. If coworkers can't see Jesus in our work, they might not be able to see why they need Jesus in their lives.

I believe that God had a good reason for creating a world where most of His children are workers instead of pastors, priests, and missionaries. His spiritual strategy, like any good commander, is to concentrate His soldiers on the front lines, where they can overwhelm the enemy. Doug Sherman and William Hendricks paint a powerful vision of what this mission "battlefield" could look like:

> The key to bringing the culture and the Church back together; to renewing the workplace and reforming the Church; to choosing Christ as the Lord of life, rather than leaving Him out of the system—may well be a movement of people who are known for their hard work, for the excellence of their effort, for their honesty and unswerving integrity, for their concern for the rights and welfare of people, for their compliance with laws, standards, and policies, for the quality of their goods and services, for the quality of their character, for the discipline and sacrifice of their lifestyle, for putting work in its proper perspective, for their leadership among coworkers— in short, for their Christlikeness on and off the job. What could such an army of workers accomplish?[6]

Benefit #6: Work is an important way of loving and serving God.
This is the last, but probably the most important spiritual benefit to

57   *The Spiritual Benefits of Working in Business*

work. The way we are to live our lives is summed up quite nicely in Deuteronomy 6:5: "Love the LORD your God with all your heart and with all your soul and with all your strength."

The key word in that verse is *all*. We are to give our all in loving God. If we are to love our God with everything we have, we must love Him in everything we do. As our life's most predominant activity, our work can and should be an expression of our love for God. If we commit our work life to God and truly work for Him, our weekday activities can be an act of worship and service to our Lord. It won't always be easy to maintain that attitude in today's frantic marketplace, but knowing God accepts our work efforts as part of our service to Him gives us the strength and hope we need to persevere.

Think about It

❑ In what way does the curse most affect your workday? What might you do to limit its impact?

❑ Which of the six benefits of work do you find most meaningful? List some examples of how that benefit plays out in your job and review the list during your next frustrating workday.

Notes

1. Foster R. McCurley and John H. Reumann, "Work in the Providence of God," in *Work as Praise*, eds. George W. Forell and William H. Lazareth (Philadelphia: Fortress Press, 1979), 30.

2. Leland Ryken, *Work & Leisure in Christian Perspective* (Portland Ore.: Multnomah Press, 1987), 131.

3. Lou Whitworth and Joe O'Day, "The Kimray Story—Inspiration and Challenger," *Spiritual Fitness in Business*, 5 No. 12 (December, 1987): 1-5.

4. Tom Peters and Nancy Austin, *A Passion for Excellence* (New York: Random House, 1985), 206.

5. Ryken, *Work & Leisure*, 170-171.

6. Doug Sherman and William Hendricks, *Your Work Matters to God* (Colorado Springs: NavPress, 1987), 269.

5

Seeing Business As a Calling

G o into any department of any business and you will find people attempting to perform tasks for which they are ill-suited.

❑ A salesperson without people skills persists in calling on
prospects and stumbling through her memorized sales pitch. She
chose sales because that's where the "big money" is, yet she barely
brings in enough business to keep her job.

❑ When he was younger, pencil and paper were always by his side
to draw the buildings he dreamed of designing. His skyscrapers
would not be boxes of cold steel and tinted glass, but would provide a
homelike environment. However, he never received the training to
take his dreams beyond the pencil scribbles. Instead, he mops the
shop floor.

❑ The employee in MIS (Management Information Systems), who
would rather be interfacing with people than computers, showed
great promise in sales while working her way through college. A
career counselor convinced her that working with computers would
always guarantee her a job.

❑ A brilliant engineer accepts a lucrative promotion to a management position with a plush office and days filled with meetings, yet
secretly yearns to go back to the front lines. Instead, he attempts to
plan and organize for those who do the work he'd rather be doing.

Most surveys indicate that between 50 and 80 percent of working Americans occupy jobs that are wrong for them, according to human resource experts Ralph Mattson and Arthur Miller. They also found that only one out of three managers and executives appears well-matched to his or her job.[1]

Should these facts concern us in our effort to make work our ministry? After all, as long as we commit our work to God, the kind of work we do doesn't matter as long as we don't sin. Right?

Most surveys indicate that between 50 and 80 percent of working Americans occupy jobs that are wrong for them.

Mismatched Christian Workers

Under today's conventional view of ministry discussed in chapter 2, the only vocations worth spiritual consideration are the "higher callings" of becoming a pastor or a missionary. The rest of us need to find whatever work we can, preferably a job that pays well so we can support our churches and those with the higher calling.

This attitude is not uncommon in many churches, where teenagers are given little career instruction except for occasional inspirational talks urging them to consider the ministry. As a result, the percentage of Christians who are poorly matched to their work may be similar to the statisics quoted by Mattson and Miller.

What is the impact of Christians working in jobs that are not consistent with their abilities and interests? Three areas concern me.

1. Mismatched workers don't perform their work at the same level as those well-suited to their jobs. It is nearly impossible to consistently perform at a high level in work that does not tap into one's key abilities and interests.

Human resource consultant Ralph Mattson sees a night-and-day difference in work performance, depending on whether the task fits with one's gifts and abilities:

In God's economy, when we undertake activities that match our gifts, we are highly motivated and energetic. When we work on projects that do not call on our gifts, we are bored. Being a job misfit requires a kind of discipline that is very difficult to sustain. [2]

Some career experts go a step further, saying that—no matter how you define success or failure—if you do not enjoy your work, you will ultimately fail. [3]

Failure is a term no one likes to hear. Does this mean that, unless we define and find our perfect job, we'll eventually be out on the streets? No, but according to career consultant Nancy Anderson in her book, *Work with Passion*, a relationship exists between interest and productivity:

> Without productivity, a business fails. Without productivity, an employee or owner becomes dissatisfied. Productivity results from genuine interest.... You'll be productive if you *love* what you are doing. For example, if you work in a chocolate chip cookie factory and love chocolate chip cookies, you will communicate that love to the owner, your co-workers, and the customers. You'll all have fun producing a product you love personally. This applies to any product or service. (Did you ever wonder why people who are financially independent continue to work when they really don't have to? The answer is that they're having fun.) [4]

I learned about choosing work that suited me while still in school. My first summer job in high school was filling in for vacationing employees at an industrial laundry. The task I disliked most was checking in uniforms for companies that had canceled or changed their order. All day I counted dirty, smelly uniforms and pulled off name tags and other attached labels. The chemicals used to loosen the labels gave me a headache and my clumsy fingers were usually raw by the end of the day. Except for keeping count of the uniforms, I wasn't especially skilled at the work—and I constantly fought to keep my mind from wandering. It took great concentration to approach the productivity standards set for the position (most weeks I fell a little short). Every 15 minutes I'd look at the clock and tell myself how much money I was making for college.

Seven summers later, I worked for the same company, this time writing an employee handbook to tell new workers about the firm. This would be the organization's first written handbook, so I assembled all the company goals, rules, and policies. I rarely looked at the clock that summer. Nearly every aspect of the project was fun for me, and I was sorry to see the work end. The manual, bound and complete with illustrations from a cartoonist I knew, became a prototype for handbooks throughout the organization. Doing something related to my abilities and interests made all the difference in my performance at work.

2. Mismatched workers face greater obstacles to being strong on-the-job witnesses for Christ. This drawback is, in part, caused by the previous one, because poor workers make poor witnesses. It is important to understand that what the non-Christian sees most from us is our work. Who is most likely, all other things being equal, to attract interest in his or her testimony—the top-selling, enthusiastic salesperson or one who is in the middle of the pack? The state's teacher of the year or "Mr. Sominex" in Chemistry? The best computer whiz in MIS or the computer hack who muddles through the day?

Like it or not, a job well done attracts attention. "Do you see a man skilled in his work? He will serve before kings; he will not serve before obscure men" (Prov. 22:29). Why are prominent businesspeople and athletes frequent speakers at outreach events? We respect those who have successfully applied their God-given gifts in this world. We are willing to listen to them, hoping to learn the "secret" to their success.

Paul Douglas, who used to be our local weatherman, was a frequent speaker at evangelistic events and outreach lunches. People came to hear him speak because of his ability to make the weather interesting. I have never enjoyed the weather more than when I watched Paul give his forecast from the station's "backyard," wowing me with computer weather mapping graphics that made me feel as if I were following the storm.

This man had neither the great looks nor the smoothness of your typical TV talking head. He was a weather "nerd." Paul got excited over any weather situation and gave viewers that extra bit of information, no matter how trivial. Weather was his passion. He gave speeches about it, wrote books and articles about it, and even started a company to sell his sophisticated mapping software to television stations throughout the country.

Because viewers saw Paul's passion for weather every night on the news, they were open to hearing him speak of his primary passion: Jesus Christ.

Non-Christians searching for answers often start by looking at those around them who appear to have their act together. In the workplace, "together" people are likely to perform their jobs well without burning out, know their strengths and limitations, have unwaivering values, and be willing to help anyone who is struggling. Workers ill-suited to their careers face a stiff challenge to be viewed as that sort of person.

3. Mismatched workers are often poor stewards of the talents and passions that God has provided. Each of us has at least one inherent ability that we can develop and draw on to make a living for ourselves and our families. Deuteronomy 8:17-18 reminds us that this capacity to make a living comes from God:

> You may say to yourself, "My power and the strength of my hands have produced this wealth for me." But remember the LORD your God, for it is He who gives you the ability to produce wealth, and so confirms His covenant, which He swore to your forefathers, as it is today.

Everything we accomplish in this world comes about because God has given us a unique mixture of natural abilities and spiritual gifts. In 1 Peter 4:10, each Christian is instructed to "use whatever gift he has received to serve others."

If God has given abilities to everyone, why is it that some people appear so talented and successful while others don't? According to Mattson and Miller, those differences are caused more by poor stewardship than by uneven distribution of talents:

> **Everything we accomplish in this world comes about because God has given us a unique mixture of natural abilities and spiritual gifts.**

The incompetency we see everywhere is not because people

lack gifts, but because they are not in the right place for their gifts. They are not being stewards of what God has given them. There are plenty of gifts to do all the work that needs to be done everywhere and to do it all gloriously well—so well, in fact, that people would go rejoicing from day to day over how much was accomplished and how well it was accomplished. But the world's systems, corrupted by the sin of man, place enormous obstacles in the way of each person who attempts to find his rightful place in creation. Such systems assume that people and creation are mere fodder for their intentions. [5]

We are imperfect people laboring in an imperfect marketplace, making it more difficult to find work well-suited to our abilities and interests. That doesn't mean all is hopeless, however. It means God wants us to work hard at being the best possible stewards of our talents.

Reviewing my own stewardship of talents is a humbling experience. Despite some success in developing my business and marketing skills, I've been a bit of a late bloomer in developing two other abilities: teaching and writing. I didn't even know I had any teaching ability until I took advantage of a one-shot opportunity to teach an adult Sunday School class at the age of twenty-seven. It took me by surprise to feel the Holy Spirit working powerfully through me, a first-time teacher, and to be strongly affirmed by so many in the class I taught. Despite the encouraging start, it was six years before I taught my first college evening course and began teaching more regularly in church.

Writing, on the other hand, was something I aspired to do since I first started writing stories in fourth grade. Except for occasional flurries of sustained writing activity, such as a three-year stint on the college newspaper staff, I've constantly battled to make time in my busy schedule for writing.

It is frustrating to have underused and underdeveloped abilities inside us that could be used to serve others. When we let our God-given abilities lie dormant and undeveloped, we risk comparison to the man in the Parable of the Talents, who buried his master's money instead of putting it to good use. Squandering what God has provided us, whether money or ability, shows little respect for the One who created us.

Historically, business management has been slow to catch on to the intricacies of God's design for humans as it relates to work. For example, the early industrial assembly line treated the worker as a mere commodity. Each place in the line required (and, in many places, still does) doing a relatively simple task over and over and over again. Anyone could be trained to perform the task in a matter of minutes, so when a laborer got sick or quit, someone else was quickly inserted.

Contrast the industrial assembly line with God's creation. Think about how the elements of a common lake ecosystem fit together. The various forms of fish, birds, mammals, insects, and plant life all have a task to perform to keep the system, and the food chain, functioning. The system is so complex and delicate that any time man adds too much of something (pollution) or subtracts something (too much fishing), every part of it is affected.

I believe that God meant for human communities to be similar. Look at the differences in each person's body build, ways of thinking, natural abilities, and range of interests. If God had intended people to be interchangeable parts, why did He bother to make each one so different?

Although the Bible doesn't answer that question for all mankind, it does tell why God made differences in Christians. Notice the term used to describe His church: the *body* of Christ. That God likens each believer to a part of the body is significant. A body has many different parts, each connected with and dependent on one another for survival. Also, body parts are not very interchangeable. A heart is good for little else than pumping blood, and ears can do nothing but hear. Each part doing its job is necessary for the body to be healthy and ready to carry out God's purpose.

In 1 Corinthians 12, Paul describes the different spiritual gifts, noting that the Holy Spirit assigns particular gifts to each Christian. The reason for this diversity is to keep the body functioning at its best, as described in verses 18-20:

> But in fact God has arranged the parts in the body, every one of them, just as He wanted them to be. If they were all one part, where would the body be? As it is, there are many parts, but one body.

In addition to being assigned a part in the body of Christ, God created each believer for specific acts of service. Paul writes in Ephesians 2:10 that Christians are "God's workmanship, created in Christ Jesus to do good works, which God prepared in advance for us to do."

As Christians, then, we are doubly equipped for our work. As humans we are born with natural abilities that surface and develop as we mature. When we accept Christ in our heart as our Lord, we receive supernatural gifts to perform the ministry God intends for us. Our work can and should be part of that ministry.

For example, if you are given the gifts of mercy and exhortation, imagine how many workers you could help with their problems. What a compassionate and loving manager you could be!

Viewing Our Work As a Calling

To see work as ministry is one thing, but to view it as a vocation, something people are called to, is another matter. Today, a common belief about calling is that all Christians receive a call to salvation, an invitation to be part of God's kingdom. A few people also receive a calling to a vocational ministry—that is, to be a pastor, missionary, or some other position in a ministry organization.

For years that was my understanding of the term *calling*. I didn't feel any sense of calling in my work, even after being in the business world for a while. In fact, because of my increasing desire to serve God, I wondered if I might be on the verge of a vocational call to ministry. I even took a couple of seminary courses in the evening to test the waters.

It was in one of those seminary classes that I clarified my calling in a way I hadn't anticipated. Phillip Frasier taught me in "Ministry of the Laity" that it is the "lay" person who is truly on the front lines of ministry. Biblically, the role of the pastor is to equip the rest of us for that ministry. This new understanding triggered an answer to the question I had been asking God for some time: "Lord, where do You want me to serve You?"

While walking to my car from class one night, I felt a clear answer from God coming from deep inside. "I want you to serve Me right where you are, in the marketplace." Years ago, I had chosen my career largely because of what I perceived to be my abilities and interests. Now I realized that God, the giver of those gifts, had called me to use them for His glory. And those gifts are best utilized in the marketplace, not the pulpit.

Does God really have a vocation for those of us who won't be pastoring a church? God's callings in the Bible do not always concern priestly matters. Sometimes His calling brought forth political or military leaders (Moses, Gideon, Saul, David) or even skilled artists to create for God's tabernacle (Ex. 31:1-6).

In the New Testament, mention of the term *calling* seems to encompass a Christian's whole life. In 1 Corinthians 7:20-24, Paul exhorts his reader to "remain in the situation God called him to."

God calls us, not just to salvation, but to a life of ministry that He has strategically mapped out for us. Dr. David McKenna, president of Asbury Theological Seminary, teaches there are three aspects to "our biblical vocation." First, we are called to salvation; then we are "commissioned to exercise our special gifts." Finally, we are consecrated to a specific work task or situation. [6]

The familiar phrase from a spiritual tract—God loves you and has a wonderful plan for your life—contains more truth than many of us realize. That plan is not limited to our eternal destination at life's conclusion, with a couple joyful Sunday mornings thrown in to make the wait tolerable. He created us as unique beings because He has a specific purpose for our lives and work.

What makes our work a true vocation then? I see two elements as critical. First, we must commit our work to God and treat it as part of our service to God. Also, we must do our best to develop and apply the gifts God has given us to our work ministry. When we reach a point where our work is a good fit with the way God designed us, our witness will be strengthened, for we will stand in stark contrast to the rest of the mismatched workforce.

> **When we reach a point where our work is a good fit with the way God designed us, our witness will be strengthened, for we will stand in stark contrast to the rest of the mismatched workforce.**

Chariots of Fire, one of my favorite movies, illustrates vocation through the story of 1924 Olympic track hero and missionary Eric Liddell. In explaining his decision to delay his mission trip until after the Olympics, Liddell said, "I believe that God made me for a purpose, for China. But He also made me fast and when I run I feel His pleasure."

Have you ever felt God's pleasure when you've done something well? I believe those feelings point to our areas of calling. In my own case, my strongest sense of God's pleasure comes when I accomplish something in areas related to my core abilities: when watching a television commercial that resulted from my marketing direction, or when teaching a class where students get excited about applying the lesson to their lives.

Finding Your Work Calling

What if our current work never seems to bring any sense of pleasure or uses pitifully little of our God-given abilities? If we number among the mismatched majority in the marketplace, how do we discover our true calling?

The answer is simple to say but more difficult to do: look at how God has made you. Ideally, the output of our labors should be a reflection of who we are, just as God's work (and Christ's) reflects His nature.

Each and every Christian is God's unique masterpiece, with different gifts and a distinct testimony of divine working in his or her life. We are custom-made instruments to do God's work in the world. Yet even the best tools are ineffective when used inappropriately. Who would try to hold together last month's two-inch thick sales report with a tiny paperclip? Or hang a picture in the office using a sledge hammer? Why should human tools be treated differently?

Because we are God's instruments, our design reflects the kind of activities He intends for us to do. Those seeking God's will for their career direction should not only look to the Lord in prayer, but also take a long inward search.

Unearthing Your Strengths

The shelves in bookstores are lined with titles to assist those needing career guidance. The best of these volumes are invaluable, although the thorough reader could easily spend weeks going through all the exercises. For those who want or need to devote that much time to their career search, I've included a short list of my favorite career books in the chapter notes.[7] Those more pressed for time may want to try this simple exercise, which has helped greatly in keeping my own career in focus.

Step one is to list all your life's achievements on a piece (or several pages) of paper, starting as far back as you can remember. You may want to break up your list into life stages, such as birth through early school years, high school/college, early career years, etc.

I would encourage you to spend extra time jotting down your early achievements, because people often express their truest nature when they are very young. For example, my business interests emerged early. By the time I reached the age of 14, I had launched four tiny business ventures, including a neighborhood carnival and a newspaper. I have vivid memories of handprinting copies of the newspaper using a pencil and sheets of carbon paper, then selling the copies to other children for a nickel.

Also, it is very important to list accomplishments beyond those that relate to your career. Why? I remember hearing a wise career counselor say that it is almost impossible to completely avoid using our strongest gifts at some point in our lives. Therefore, mismatched workers might discover their gifts in hobbies, sports, church activities, games, reading topics, etc. Winning a fly-fishing competition, growing the best vegetables in the neighborhood, or raising lots of money for a local charity might offer clues as to the type of work you'd enjoy.

Step two. Once you've made a list of your life's major and minor accomplishments (at least two dozen), go back and put a star in front of those achievements of which you are especially proud. Then go through the list again, this time circling those activities you enjoyed the most.

At this point, you should have a handful of accomplishments that are both starred and circled. You should examine and compare these closely, because they should provide some idea as to the work situations where you would thrive and the abilities you are motivated to use—motivated because the task is something you enjoy doing and do well.

Often it takes only a little information to guide us in the right direction. Landscaping business owner Jim Bever saw very early in his career that the only jobs he enjoyed were those where he could spend time outdoors. That information led him to make choices, like driving a delivery truck instead of working inside, where he said he felt like a caged tiger. On his truck route, Jim started selling plants to the customers he visited. Many of those who bought plants sought his advice on how to arrange them in their yard to look attractive. Before long, he was in business.

Understanding of my own work abilities and preferences has evolved over time. Looking over my accomplishments, I saw that business activities and writing were visible at every stage in my life. Adding that up with my high school debate/oratory competitions and years of political involvement, I saw a pattern. I love working with ideas. I especially enjoy influencing the thinking and actions of others. My optimal work environment seems to require both time for independent work/thinking, as well as opportunities to discuss ideas and brainstorm with others. With that understanding, it isn't difficult to figure out why I am attracted to marketing, writing, and teaching.

Knowing what situations, abilities, and environments lead to our best achievements is a critical first step toward finding and following our work calling. Here are some additional tips to keep your career journey on track.

1. Identify your spiritual gifts. When people invite Jesus to be Lord of their life, the Holy Spirit enters their heart and begins to change them. All believers receive gifts of the Spirit to help them in their ministry. Since we know from the Bible that ministry includes everyday work, discovering and developing our spiritual gifts can help us clarify our vocational purpose.

For anyone unfamiliar with the concept of spiritual gifts, 1 Corinthians 12, Romans 12, and 1 Peter 4:10-11 offer some instruction. Most of the teaching I've had regarding spiritual gifts assumes that the local church is the sole outlet for using them. There is some truth to that, since the gifts are meant to build up the body of Christ—and churches are its key institutions. Yet the

Bible does not put a tight restriction on the use of these gifts. First Peter 4:10 tells the Christian to "use whatever gift he has received to serve others, faithfully administering God's grace in its various forms."

"To serve others" is a good guideline as to how to use our gifts, and our jobs should certainly be part of that. If one has a strong gift of teaching, leading a Sunday School class once a week needn't be the full extent of using that gift. Many Christians have made a substantial and lasting impact on children teaching in both public and private schools. Others have made an equally significant contribution teaching adults in college and corporate training programs.

The gift of mercy can be applied to many job fields, health care being the first one I think about. In our health care organization, I found that the real spiritual comforting in a hospital doesn't always come from a hospital chaplain, since nurses, social workers, therapists, and others have many hours of caring contact with patients.

Discussions of spiritual gifts can be confusing. Is it important, for example, to know whether a particular ability we have is natural or spiritual. Well, both kinds of gifts come from God, one given when we are born and another when the Holy Spirit enters our hearts. Also, the two kinds of gifts are closely related to one another. Mattson and Miller report that they have never seen Christians with spiritual gifts which are not in harmony with, or an extension of, their natural gifts. [8]

A key to making our work ministry effective is to find, develop, and apply all the gifts God has given us to use for His glory and service.

2. Don't be afraid to follow your passions and interests. The word passion is not used frequently in religious books, possibly because of its frequent association with lustful sins of the flesh. Yet, passion, and its synonym *enthusiasm*, is exactly the sort of feeling we should be seeking in our work.

The word *enthusiasm*, by the way, comes from two Greek words, *en* and *theos*, meaning "God within us" or "inspired by God." In earlier times, Christians were taught that enthusiasm meant God was working in your heart attracting you to an activity. Today, those emotions are often downplayed, as many of us suspect that anything enjoyable is either sinful, fattening, or carcinogenic.

Anything touted as "good for us" is thought to be boring or difficult. My physician, in prescribing exercise for my good health, put it this way, "If it's boring, it must be good for you."

Applying this approach to work is dangerous because we begin to believe that work and enjoyment are mutually exclusive activities. According to Richard Bolles, author of the best-selling *What Color Is Your Parachute?* that is not what God intends:

> Enjoyment, in human life, isn't a fluke. It's part of God's plan. God wants us to eat; therefore God designs us so that eating is enjoyable. God wants us to sleep; therefore God designs us so that sleeping is enjoyable. God wants us to procreate, love, and make love; therefore God designs us so that sex is enjoyable, and love even more so. God gives us unique (or at least unusual) skills and talents; therefore God designs us so that, when we use them, they are enjoyable. [9]

Thus, God has given us the means to make work more enjoyable: our talents. Those talents also provide a pleasant means of putting food on the table. In fact, if you look at top people in any field—the most respected and most accomplished in what they do—you'll probably find people who enjoy their work.

Before I met actor Tony Randall, I'd heard him quoted as saying he couldn't believe people paid him to do what he loved, that he would've paid others just to let him act. I never gave his statement much thought. After all, who wouldn't enjoy being a television star?

I saw him when he came to speak at a local convention for older adults. One of our company's administrators was to introduce him to the crowd, so Tony whisked her aside to prepare her. He went over what she should say and instructed her to take a drink of water while at the podium, all to set up his opening line: "Thank you for that eloquent introduction and the used water."

For an accomplished actor, a brief speech to people in a faraway town could hardly be considered a career highlight. His passion for acting, however, made the event enjoyable for himself and everyone attending.

Can running a business arouse the same sort of passion? It certainly has that potential for people working in a position that matches their interests and abilities.

I never had to convince my wife Kathy that I have a passion for marketing. She sees it every time we go to the supermarket. Unsupervised, I can easily spend an hour or longer meandering down each aisle with my shopping cart, marveling at the array of new products on the shelves. For instance, I was intrigued when the first nonfrozen microwave dinners came out. Cooking time could be saved, since the food didn't have to defrost. Also, the risk of having a partially burned, partially frozen dinner could be eliminated. Perhaps only those with a passion for marketing or food could get excited over a meal in a box (although I recall my enthusiasm waned after the first taste).

If nothing in your present job excites you even a little, perhaps it would be wise to identify what does enthuse you and find ways of incorporating those activities into your work life. This may be a time-consuming task for those who have done passionless work for many years, because your work interests may be hard to recall. You might need to set up a retreat to take an in-depth look at your potential work passions.

> **If nothing in your present job excites you even a little, perhaps it would be wise to identify what does enthuse you and find ways of incorporating those activities into your work life.**

3. Be realistic and patient. At some point in reading this chapter, perhaps your mind wandered to a daydream about the ideal job for you, one that is a perfect fit with your interests and abilities.

Now take a look through the employment section of the Sunday newspaper. Most likely, that ideal job isn't listed. And some of the positions advertised might not be ideal for anybody. In our imperfect and sinful world, jobs aren't always tailored to meet the needs of individual workers, and mismatched employees often occupy positions that would be ideal for someone else.

Even in an imperfect business world, however, most of us can create work better suited to our abilities and interests. It requires patience, persistence and a little bit of creativity to bring about such a change. Sometimes it can happen without leaving your current employer.

73   *Seeing Business As a Calling*

My marketing position at HealthEast, for instance, used many of my marketing skills, but little of my writing, teaching, and entrepreneurial interests. When another manager left the department back in 1991, I successfully proposed a department restructuring that allowed me to work there just three days a week. That opened up two extra days for me to pursue those other interests—and I thank God nearly every day for that opportunity. I still haven't reached my "ideal" work situation, but I'm a lot closer to it than I was five years ago.

A Tough Question

Finally, if someone is stuck in a job ill-suited for him or her, can that work still be an effective ministry? First of all, the number of people who are truly "stuck" in a particular job until retirement is probably very small. Even the most stuck people I know—those with family members whose pre-existing health condition keeps them from switching employers without losing health insurance coverage—can still seek new positions within their existing companies. Most of the time, we mistake "stuck" for being unable to get by on even a few dollars less income, or being unwilling to arrange time priorities to explore new skills, or being reluctant to have others think we've lost our mind for giving up such a respectable position.

Paul's address to slaves in Colossians 3:22-25, referred to previously, tells those working in bondage that it is Jesus Christ they are serving. So, yes, our least favorite job can still be a ministry. However, Paul would probably not approve of being stuck in such a job unless necessary. In 1 Corinthians 7:21, he writes, "Were you a slave when you were called? Don't let it trouble you—although if you can gain your freedom, do so."

The freedom to sharpen our talents, to become the tool God intended, is to be eagerly sought and cherished. Our ministry at work can be much more effective and rewarding when the task before us is part of our calling, not just our duty.

Think about It

❑ On a scale of one to ten, how "mismatched" are you with your work? How can you become better matched? (List specific tasks and responsibilities.)

❑ What kind of work do you think God has called you to? If you have trouble answering this question, consider working through the exercise in this chapter or seeking out one of the additional resources listed in the footnotes.

Notes

1. Ralph Mattson and Arthur Miller, *Finding a Job You Can Love* (Nashville: Thomas Nelson Publishers, 1982), 123.

2. Ralph Mattson, "Where Would God Have Us Work?" *Tabletalk* (August 1993): 10.

3. Richard Germann, Diane Blumenson, and Peter Arnold, *Working & Liking It* (New York: Fawcett Columbine Books, 1984), 2.

4. Nancy Anderson, *Work with Passion* (New York: Carroll & Graf Publishers Inc. and Whatever Publishing, 1984), 139.

5. Mattson and Miller, *Finding a Job You Can Love*, 41.

6. David McKenna, *Love Your Work* (Wheaton, Ill. Victor Books, 1990), 71.

7. Of the many career books out there, here are four I've found to be extremely helpful. *Finding a Job You Can Love* (see Note #1) and *The Great Niche Hunt* by David J. Frahm with Paula Rinehart (NavPress, 1991) provide good exercises for discovering your career design, yet provide a spiritual perspective. *Work with Passion* (Note #4) and the annually published *What Color Is Your Parachute?* (Note #9) also include steps on how to get the job that's right for you.

8. Mattson and Miller, *Finding a Job You Can Love*, 158.

9. Richard Nelson Bolles, *The 1987 What Color Is Your Parachute?* (Berkeley, Calif. Ten Speed Press, 1987), 100.

Part **2**

Godly Principles That
Make Business Sense

••

In the first five chapters of this book, we've examined concepts such as ministry, spiritual significance of work, and calling from a biblical perspective. We have come to a clearer understanding that work in business can be a meaningful ministry.

The chapters in Part 2 more clearly flesh out what our ministry might look like. How should Christians treat customers and others who depend on the quality of our work? How should we act toward our bosses, our peers, our employees? How can we develop Christlike integrity on the job? What common business practices should we avoid and what should we embrace?

My hope is that you will discover something worthwhile in the coming pages that will improve the value of your work for both your heavenly and earthly superiors.

6

Provide Good Service
As God's Servants

··

T here's an old bit of wisdom that says the best way to understand a man is to walk a mile in his shoes. Some say that is
also the best way to understand how to serve the needs of
your customers. Walk in my shoes for a minute as I describe my visits to two retail establishments.

First, I pulled up to a florist in a small shopping center. On an
impulse, I had decided to surprise Kathy with a bouquet of flowers,
a little token of appreciation that always thrills her. I opened the
door and a loud bell signaled my arrival. No one was in the store,
except a woman in the back room putting together a floral arrangement. For a while I wandered around the shop browsing for just the
right item. Still no sales clerk. Then I confined my pacing to the
sales counter and the other areas of the shop that could be clearly
seen from the other room. Nothing. I even made noises, tapping my
wedding ring on the counter and moving pots around. The clerk
started working on yet another arrangement.

I was about to shout for some help, but a better idea came to me.
The grocery store next door sold flowers too, complete with cashiers
ready to serve me. As I made my final departure from the florist, I
paused to jiggle the door a few times, thinking the bells might cause
an apologetic woman to rush out to greet me. Wrong again.

My next visit was to a place that can be named without shame,
a Mail Boxes, Etc,. franchise located near my home in White Bear
Lake, Minnesota. As soon as I walked in the door, a smiling young
man behind the counter asked how he might help me.

"Just copies today," I said, holding out my hand to receive the copy counter that was instantly placed before me. As I walked toward the copiers, the clerk told me to be sure to ask if I needed any assistance.

I quickly returned to the sales counter, because I only needed to make a few copies. I pulled a prepaid copy card out of my wallet, which I had purchased a few months ago at a discount. The clerk hesitated when he saw my card. "Did you know this is customer appreciation month? Right now, the price for copies is less than you paid for your card, so you could save money by paying cash."

> **Providing outstanding service to our customers at work is one of the best means of service to God.**

I was grateful for the advice, even though my total order was under a dollar. In fact, I rarely spend more than a couple of bucks when I visit Mail Boxes, Etc., but the people there always treat me like a VIP. Because I matter to them, I'll gladly keep coming back.

These contrasting examples of customer service raise a few questions. Which company is more likely to be run by Christians? Should Christians be held to a higher standard of service than other workers? Could Christians feel good about their work ministry if the flower shop example were typical of the kind of service they provide?

In this chapter, I contend that providing outstanding service to our customers at work is one of the best means of service to God. In Mark 10:42-45, Christ told us to be servants of all. Paul's instruction in Philippians 2:3-4 continues along this vein, saying we should consider others to be better than ourselves (a way of countering our natural self-centeredness). Therefore, each Christian "should look not only to your own interests, but also to the interests of others."

One of those "others" for which all businesses exist to serve is the customer. For the Christian, doing an outstanding job in meeting customer needs is both an effective service to God and also a substantial benefit to the company.

Why Is Good Service So Important?

Some of you may ask the question: aren't businesses already providing good service? After all, countless books, articles, and seminars drive the service theme into the heads of executives everywhere. Customer and market survey results could fill a small library at some firms. What company would ever state in their annual report: "We won't be providing any customer service next year"?

Before I go any further, it might be useful to define what I mean by customer service. At its most basic and minimum level, customer service is simply meeting customers' needs and expectations. Needs are what people are coming to us or our company to fulfill and expectations are how they expect those needs to be met.

Despite all the talk about customer service, most businesses, at best, only do an average job of meeting minimum levels of customer needs and expectations. Even when our surveys show that customers are satisfied, we need to understand that, because of past experiences, their expectation levels are not lofty. What do you expect when you walk into a large discount store? Low prices, empty shelves where the hot sale items are supposed to be, merchandise of varying quality, and scarce sales help.

With those expectations, what happens when a company does something extra? Wal-Mart puts an outgoing employee at the front door to greet each entering shopper. It surprises people, exceeds their expectations, and generally increases customer loyalty. In a survey of 70 U.S. retail chains, Wal-Mart was ranked fourth in terms of friendly store employees. Their main competitors, K Mart and Target, came in 31st and 33rd.[1]

Great customer service is not just meeting customer needs and expectations, it's exceeding them. Companies do not build loyalty by merely satisfying customers' lowest expectations, but rather by wooing and wowing them. Wooing means letting them know they are valued and wowing means providing something the customer values before anyone else thinks to do it.

Saturn has shown the automobile industry that wooing and wowing potential buyers requires more substance than rebates, spotlights, and floating big, helium-filled animals over a dealership. In fact, Saturn's success may have more to do with how they treat their customers than even the cars they make. Think about your worst car-buying episode as you read this part of their business philosophy:

> To be truly successful, our sights must be aimed beyond providing customer satisfaction; we must exceed customer expec-

tations and provide an unparalleled buying and vehicle-ownership experience that results in customer enthusiasm.[2]

Saturn talked with consumers, who told them what they didn't like about the experience of buying a car: pushy salespeople, misleading prices, and the need to negotiate nearly every aspect of the purchase. These were considered necessary evils in buying a vehicle. No longer. Even competing dealerships are beginning to experiment with the Saturn sales experience —hiring salaried sales consultants and charging the same price to each customer.

Despite encouraging stories like Saturn's, most businesses still haven't gotten the point. According to management consultant and author Milind Lele, businesses choose between two primary strategies to keep a jump on the competition: cut costs or maximize customer satisfaction. Despite the fact that most companies talk about both of these strategies, Lele asserts that one approach will dominate:

> Cutting costs and maximizing customer satisfaction are not two sides of the same coin. The two goals demand different approaches to product design, to manufacturing, to sales—in short, to every aspect of the firm's operations. The first strategy says, "We will produce and market a parity product—one that performs as well as most competitors' offerings—more efficiently than any of our adversaries." The second strategy says, "Customers will pay more for a product that really makes them happy, so let's find out what that product is and how we can make it with reasonable efficiency." [3]

Which strategy do most firms use? Cutting costs. And which strategy do the most profitable, successful firms in nearly every industry use? Studies of top business performers conducted by Lele, McKinsey and Co., the Strategic Planning Institute's PIMS (Profit Impact of Market Strategy) data, and the Peters and Waterman research published in *In Search of Excellence* all have similar conclusions: nearly every firm at the top of its field has an emphasis on customer service, providing superior value to their customers. [4]

Just about every company talks about serving the customer, yet each of us still experiences service nightmares in hotels, restau-

82

rants, with retailers, and with vendors we use at work. Why the discrepancy? The answer is that many business owners and managers believe in customer service and know it works, but are not *committed* to making it the top priority, to making the investment of time and money necessary to bring it about.

The difference between belief and commitment is perhaps best illustrated by a close look at Christianity in the United States. For years studies have shown that a very high percentage of Americans say they believe in God. This contrasts with signs that the country is moving away from traditional, Christian values: rising crime, crumbling families, morals/values that are now man-based instead of God-based, scores of empty churches, and a growing hostility among many to the Gospel message.

The Bible teaches that believing God exists is useless without commitment, without placing God first in one's life. James 2:19 puts it best: "You believe that there is one God. Good! Even the demons believe that—and shudder."

The first commandment also says we are to have no other gods before God. If Jesus Christ is not the center of our life—if He is second in priority to ourselves, our work, our family, or some other god—then our "faith" is worthless and the only fruit our life will bear won't even be good enough for the compost heap.

Most companies believe in providing good customer service, just as long as it doesn't cost very much or take much time or cut into this quarter's profit margin. When the economy goes a little soft, customer service programs and training are tempting targets for cutbacks. Employees who provide customer service get the message: customer service is nice, but what we really value is keeping costs down.

Top companies, however, have a much deeper commitment to serving the customer. They are "on fire" about customer service, much like new converts when they accept Christ into their lives. They don't just try to keep customers satisfied, they want buyers to love their company. They want customers who'll tell everyone they know to try their products or services.

Intuit, maker of Quicken®, the runaway best-selling personal finance computer program, is just such a company. The massive sales force that vaulted Quicken® to the top of the heap does not appear on the payroll. According to founder and president Scott

Cook, the goal is to create "apostles" of sorts, making "the customer feel so good about the product they'll [sic] go and tell five friends to buy it." [5]

In many leading companies, "what the customer wants" is treated as gospel-truth, with outstanding customer service being the primary means of business "evangelism." Is this fervor something Christians should embrace or back away from?

For many of those in the business world, the customer service focus does not represent a newfound bent toward altruism. As business thinking and research have progressed, they've finally learned that treating customers right is the most profitable route in the long run. The carrot hung before them—their motive—is still the same: making more money. Now they've found a way to reach their goal without feeling guilty about how they got there.

Today, Christian workers can not only embrace serving the customer without guilt, but we can also experience extra joy and fulfillment. We can put into practice the same service principles as the others—without the carrot. Our motive is much higher. For we serve others out of a desire to serve our Lord, who came down on earth in the form of a servant to show us the way. The love of God is intended to overflow from inside us out to others.

How to Be Christ to Our Customers

The principles of great customer service are not complicated in theory, yet they are difficult to implement without concentrated, ongoing attention by everyone in the company. For Christians, the essence of service is treating our customers in a Christlike manner.

To best remember that great customer service is being Christ to those we serve, I've arranged the key elements of service into the acronym, CHRIST: Care, Hear, Respond, Invest, Surprise, Trust. Let's look at each part individually.

Care about and for customers. Caring seems like such a basic thing to do, except that it is seen so rarely in interactions with most businesses. In his books, Tom Peters uses the term *uncommon courtesy* to describe the approach of the few companies who treat people right, and he uses the term *thinly disguised contempt* to describe the others. In most firms, customers are seen as (and treated as) necessary evils.

Caring is the easiest way to share Christ's love with others. In fact, after Jesus shared the greatest commandments (love God with everything you've got and love your neighbor as yourself), He illustrated it with the Parable of the Good Samaritan. In Luke 10:30-37, the Samaritan saw the robbery victim in need, took pity on him, and "took care of him." Although the needs of our customers are usually not this grave, taking care of them is still an important part of loving our neighbor.

Outstanding businesses have been wildly successful by trying to live out a variation of the Great Commandment: treat customers as you yourself would like to be treated.

Nordstrom is perhaps the best example of great customer service in a retail setting. In a survey of seventy retail chains, Nordstrom was ranked first in customer satisfaction.[6] Those results would be of no surprise to their regular shoppers, each of whom could relate a situation where a sales clerk went the extra mile to help.

> **Caring is the easiest way to share Christ's love with others.**

Our family has a few such stories, such as when Kathy's mother asked a sales clerk if they carried a particular brand of men's dress shirt. That item wasn't in the clerk's department. She could have just directed us to the right department, but she said she'd call over there and check to save us walking halfway across the store just to ask a question (actually, the distance was less than 100 feet).

Another time, Kathy spent nearly an hour with a Nordstrom salesperson trying on dresses for an upcoming wedding. When she found the perfect dress, alas, it was not in her size. Over the next couple of days, the employee called Nordstrom stores throughout the region searching for the dress, even contacting the manufacturer's warehouse. She called us a few times to inform us of her progress and, even though her efforts were unsuccessful, we appreciated the effort.

Even though Nordstrom employees are partly compensated by commission, that is not the only factor at work here. I remember hearing of a Nordstrom employee who walked a customer across the mall to Macy's to find just the right dress.

85   *Provide Good Service As God's Servants*

Commitment to caring must be demonstrated at all levels of the organization to be effective. If top management doesn't care for the customer, it's difficult to expect frontline employees to get the message. One of our hospital units reported complaints about some nurses who were slow in answering patients' calls for assistance. The hospital administrator and associate administrator demonstrated how the problem should be solved by regularly walking down the unit hallway and stopping in on any room where the call light was lit. Employees got the message a lot faster than if administration had just sent out a memo.

Hear your customers. We all have needs and expectations when we plan to purchase something. Providers of exceptional service unearth those needs, trying to exceed expectations wherever possible. Hearing can involve typical market research activities such as surveys and focus groups, but nothing is better than direct customer contact.

The makers of Quicken® software spent loads of time and money getting input from their customers through surveys, focus groups, and endless product testing. Back in 1990, management at Intuit decided they were missing something. They had never studied people just setting up the program in their own homes. According to product manager Mari Latterell, that meant that "we didn't really know how easy it was to get started with Quicken.®"[7]

In response to that need, Intuit began a Follow-Me-Home program, where Quicken® buyers volunteered to let a company representative observe them when they first use the program. As a result of watching and listening to customers, Intuit came up with new ways to make Quicken® even easier to use.

When Seafirst Bank in Seattle tried listening to their customers, they told them banking was not their favorite activity and that parts of the process—especially applying for a loan—were intimidating. Banking was just another errand for these consumers, so convenience was their prime need. Seafirst changed their banks from top to bottom, adding items such as a customer service greeter at the entrance who can approve checks and answer questions and a toll-free customer service hotline that is answered 24 hours a day. Management made every effort to back up their new advertising slogan: "We make banking easy for you."[8]

Another service most people do not enjoy using is health care services, particularly in-patient hospital care. Until recently, many health care professionals had an air of superiority when it came to listening to their customers, who were appropriately named "patients." "We know what's best for the patient" was a common rebuff to letting the end-user have input into health services. As a result of listening, many hospitals are now trying something new called patient-focused care. They are revamping their units so more services are provided in or near the customer's room instead of transporting scantily-gowned patients all over the hospital.

At HealthEast, we made it a policy that any advertising campaign spending over $5,000 needed to have the creative concepts tested with consumers in focus groups. It only makes sense to ensure that your audience understands your message. Although ad agencies don't often relish testing rough concepts with consumers, every time we ran focus groups we ended up with ideas that improved the final advertising effort.

Hearing what customers have to say is critical to knowing how to meet their needs. Besides, responding without listening is considered "folly" and "shame" in Proverbs 18:13. James 1:19 notes that we should "be quick to listen, slow to speak and slow to become angry."

Listening is a prerequisite for worthwhile living, including the attainment of eternal life. Jesus said, "I tell you the truth, whoever hears My words and believes Him who sent Me has eternal life and will not be condemned; he has crossed over from death to life" (John 5:24).

Respond to customer needs and problems. Actually, I see three related *R*s when talking about Christlike treatment of customers: *responding* to customer needs quickly, *repenting* when a customer is dissatisfied, and *rebounding* rapidly when a mistake is made. Caring about customers and listening to them is useless unless a company is willing to respond to them. For example, if your local fast-food burger joint suddenly started asking you how you wanted your hamburger cooked, you'd expect something different than the precooked burger you're used to getting. If you received one of those well-done burgers after asking for medium rare, you'd be more upset than if no one had asked your preference.

One type of customer feedback most businesses don't like to receive is complaints about their products or services. The response is only natural—none of us like receiving bad news. Because of this, companies often don't make it easy to voice dissatisfaction. I remember a hospital complaint forms novelty item that was circulated a few years ago. The cardboard placard for the complaint form pad told patients to submit five copies to the office and be sure to include insurance group and I.D. number. Of course, the form itself was only a half-inch square. Unfortunately, real complaint procedures are often just as challenging to customers.

Have you ever tried to return an item to a store or complain about something and ended up feeling as if *you* were to blame for the problem? Organizations that truly believe the customer is always right immediately take responsibility for a customer's unhappiness and do whatever it takes to fix the problem. Retailers are finding that liberal return policies increase revenues because shoppers can buy with more confidence, knowing they don't have to live with a poor purchase.

Why do some companies spend so much money making sure problems are easily fixed? Those firms are practicing a technique called "exceptional recovery" (fixing customer problems and organizational mistakes with flare and panache), and have found that restoring good relations with an unhappy customer is one of the highest impact activities they can undertake.

In fact, a National Consumer Study conducted for the U.S. Office of Consumer Affairs found that buyers who complained and had their problems satisfactorily resolved were more likely to be "brand loyal" than consumers who had no problems at all. The now satisfied complainers were also significantly more brand loyal than those who had problems but did not complain.[9]

The lessons from this kind of research are clear. Make it easy for your customers to complain. And make sure those who take those complaints have the authority to fix the problem. For example, Xerox Corporation allows its service employees to replace up to $250,000 in equipment if customers are not getting the desired results.

Another customer-responsive strategy gaining popularity in many businesses is service guarantees. Here, some component of good service is guaranteed, meaning the company will pay the customer something if it falls short. Pizza delivery businesses like

Domino's widely promoted its "30 minutes or it's free" delivery guarantee (although they eventually changed it to $3 off). Now, even formally stodgy institutions like banks are getting into the act. Seafirst Bank introduced a five-minute service guarantee: wait longer than five minutes to get helped, and the bank immediately credits $5 to your account.

> **Jesus frequently frustrated His apostles by stopping to meet a need when they were in haste to make their schedule.**

In the hustle of running a business, it's easier to tell customers to "pardon the inconvenience" than to interrupt our all-important agenda. Jesus never did that. He frequently frustrated His apostles by stopping to meet a need when they were in haste to make their schedule. In the midst of His teaching, people brought little children to Jesus for Him to touch them and pray for them. His disciples rebuked those people. Surely the Son of God had more important tasks on His agenda. Jesus was indignant about this attitude and told His disciples not to hinder the children (Mark 10:13-16). Even while Jesus was rushing off to heal the dying daughter of Jairus (Mark 5:21-34), He was so sensitive to the needs of others that He felt the woman touch His clothing for healing, and He stopped to respond to her.

Invest in taking care of customer needs. If a business concentrates on serving the customer, it must invest heavily over the long haul to ensure continued customer satisfaction and loyalty. Many firms spend millions of marketing dollars trying to bring in new business, yet few spend even a fraction of that to keep those buyers buying.

Keeping customers buying requires investment of considerable time, energy, and money into ensuring that each contact point with the company is a positive experience. For most businesses, that may mean investing in their frontline employees—and anyone else who may encounter customers. This people investment is critical. The leader of a "Guerrilla Selling" workshop I attended, noting a study of why customers stop buying, said that 68 percent leave because of an attitude of indifference on the part of an employee.

Mail-order giant Lands' End has gone all out to ensure that their catalog shoppers have no reasons to buy elsewhere. None of the telephone order takers answer a call without a minimum of seventy-five hours of training. Those salespeople have every item of the catalog within reach so they are better able to answer questions, and the lines are staffed with enough people so that, on average, a caller only has to wait two rings before talking to a live person. Salespeople are backed up by specialty shoppers, who can answer more technical questions or help coordinate a new wardrobe. The main computer system is backed up by an uninterruptible power supply (so callers will never hear, "the computer is down"), and is upgraded as often as every year so that the increasing number of callers know instantly what items are in stock and that their order will be shipped within 24 hours. Founder Gary Comer explains the Lands' End philosophy:

> "Think small" is our credo. Worry about being better, bigger will take care of itself. Think one customer at a time and take care of each one the best way you can. [10]

Investment in serving the customer is even more difficult in today's era of corporate downsizing since customer service programs and employee training are often attractive targets for shortsighted expense cutting. In fact, hard times are a good indicator of how serious a company views service because, when profits have vanished, any expense that is not a core part of the organization will disappear too.

Ritz-Carlton Hotels, the first hospitality organization to win the Malcolm Baldrige National Quality Award, puts customer service and employee service training at the top of its priority list. Each employee in the hotel chain receives a minimum of 100 hours of training annually, which includes 15-minute "line-up" mini-sessions that begin every employee's day. President Horst Schulze is a participant in new employee training. His customer service message is: "You are more important to customers than I am. If you don't show up, we are in trouble. If I don't show up, hardly anyone would notice."[11]

How well does the Ritz-Carlton service message hold up during tough times? During a recent economic downturn, President

Schulze made an order as to who was off-limits in terms of layoffs. Number one on that list was the training manager.

Let's not forget the example of the best trainer in history: Jesus Christ. Despite all the demands for His time, Jesus continued to focus the bulk of His efforts on training the disciples to carry on after Him. In fact, Matthew 11:1 indicates that Jesus delayed much of His public teaching and preaching until *after* He had finished instructing His twelve disciples. Spending time to build up others is an important part of our ministry.

Surprise customers by exceeding their expectations. One of the ways we can make our customers feel a little better about life (and about our company) is to give them something extra they didn't think they could get. Providing surprises for customers can create immense excitement and loyalty for the products and services your business provides.

As I mentioned earlier in the chapter, most people do not have very high expectations for many of their day-to-day transactions. For me, few services held lower expectations than automotive repair. Knowing next-to-nothing about the workings of an engine, I have always been at the mercy of the mechanic's judgment. Much of my repair experience has been with automotive dealer service centers or other large chain outfits, whose mechanics always seemed to find expensive problems on every visit, even when all I wanted was my oil changed.

When Kathy and I moved to White Bear Lake, we started taking our aging vehicles to a tiny repair shop called Bellaire Motors, mainly because it was within walking distance. I remember an early visit with my 11-year-old Honda Accord, which was not running properly. A mechanic called me and said he had located the problem, which could only be repaired at a Honda dealership.

When I picked up my car, I asked what I owed. "Nothing," was the reply. "We didn't repair anything, so we didn't charge anything." Given past dealings with repair shops, this treatment genuinely surprised me. I don't know if that is their regular practice, but the free visit told me they intended to treat me fairly. Is it any wonder why they receive most of our lucrative fix-it business, and why they are usually swamped with the neighborhood's automobiles?

One of the keys to outstanding customer service is figuring out customer hot buttons that will create excitement and loyalty for your particular product or service. Here are a few examples of simple improvements that generated a lot of buyer enthusiasm.

❑ Airlines created frequent flier programs to attempt to gain repeat business. At Southwest Airlines, frequent fliers are regularly invited to assist in the auditioning and selection of flight attendants. Some members even take time off from work to help out. "Why not do it?" one member commented. "It's my airline." [12]

❑ People who are not computer whizzes view the "easy to use" claim with suspicion because it makes them feel stupid when it takes them hours or days to begin using a program. Quicken's® surprise factor is that it really is easy to use. To overcome the suspicion, the folks at Intuit had to come up with something more specific. "You'll be using Quicken® in six minutes or it's free" became a promotional theme that turned people into believers.

❑ College graduates usually dread getting phone calls from their alma mater because the purpose usually involves asking for contributions. The University of Utah concluded a successful fund-raising campaign by calling back all contributors just to thank them for helping the school reach its goal—without asking for additional money.

❑ Health care customers often say not waiting to see the doctor would be a pleasant surprise. Although I've yet to discover such a clinic, my dentist's waiting room is often empty. In nine years of annual visits, I've spent a total of five minutes in the waiting area. And my dentist does all the work himself, including the cleaning.

❑ In *A Passion for Excellence*, the authors call customer surprises "Kleenex-box experiences," named for a resort that won over ski enthusiasts by simply placing a box of tissues at the head of the lift line so people could wipe their goggles as they headed up the slope. [13]

Jesus was also a pleasant surprise to the people of Israel, compared to the other religious leaders of that day. Notice how many times in the Gospel of Matthew that those around Him were "amazed" or "astonished": after delivering the Sermon on the

Mount (7:28), calming the storm (8:27), healing the blind man and the demon-possessed mute (9:33), teaching about the rich and the Kingdom of God (19:25), and answering the questions about paying taxes to Caesar (22:22).

One of the most useful activities we can perform in business is to search for those little surprises that let customers know we care about them and their needs. In each industry those surprises may take a different form. What doesn't differ, however, is the appreciation people feel when companies strive to break out of the "me-too" sameness and mediocrity most customers face.

Trust is vital to any business relationship. Just as trust needs to exist in human relationships, every time someone buys a product or service a certain level of trust is required. Trust is built when the item or service purchased performs as promised/advertised. Trust is broken, sometimes permanently, when performance is below expectations or if a customer feels deceived by unfulfilled promises.

Trust is an important aspect of our Christian witness. Just as we are to trust in the Lord completely (Prov. 3:5), His workers are also to show we can be fully trusted so we "will make the teaching about God our Savior attractive" (Titus 2:10).

A key aspect of customer trust is its fragility. A hospital system once acquired a suburban hospital where a previous owner had strongly emphasized keeping operating costs at rock-bottom levels. Sparse staffing levels fueled concerns by some community members, who lost confidence in the facility. Despite new owners, dedicated employees, adequate staffing, and an image-building campaign, the hospital eventually closed its doors. Although other market factors contributed to its closure, the hospital never regained the level of trust and community support it had during its early years.

Some companies will go to great extremes to maintain the trust of those they serve. Maytag faced such a trust situation back in the 1950s when some of its steel suppliers were temporarily shut down. The company had a decision to make: use cheaper foreign steel which did not have the rust-preventing zinc coating they had always insisted on having or lose sales and profits by scaling back production until its suppliers could again deliver. Maytag's leadership decided that even a short-term compromise in product quality was not worth a possible permanent loss of consumer trust.

Showing Christ's Love to Customers

Being a genuine servant to customers, both internal and external, is a great way to follow Christ's command to serve others in love. Besides creating happy customers, the loving servant also becomes a clear beacon of light for Christ in a marketplace filled with indifference and selfishness. Christians dedicated to the needs of their customers can feel good about carrying out an important ministry in furthering the kingdom of God.

Think about It

❏ What are five specific ways you can become a better servant tomorrow to your customers or to others who depend on your work?

Notes

1. Joy Cyndee Miller, "Nordstrom is Tops in Survey," *Marketing News* (15 February 1993): 12–13.

2. Dorothy Cottrell, Larry Davis, Pat Detrick, and Marty Raymond, "Sales Training and the Saturn Difference," *Training & Development* (December 1992): 40.

3. Milind M. Lele and Jagdish N. Sheth, *The Customer Is Key* (New York: John Wiley & Sons, 1987), 8.

4. Tom Peters and Nancy Austin, *A Passion for Excellence* (New York: Random House, 1985), 52–53.

5. John Case, "Customer Service: The Last Word," *Inc.* (April 1991): 90.

6. Miller, "Nordstrom Is Tops," 12.

7. Case, "Customers Service," 91.

8. Milo Paich, "Making Service Quality Look Easy," *Training* (February 1992): 32-35

9. Ron Zemke, "Creating Customer Value," *Training* (September 1993): 47.

10. Ron Zemke and Dick Schaaf, *The Service Edge* (New York: New American Library, 1989), 385.

11. Patricia A. Galagan, "Putting on the Ritz," *Training & Development* (December 1993): 42.

12. James L. Heskett, Thomas O. Jones, Gary W. Loveman, W. Earl Sasser, Jr., and Leonard A. Schlesinger, "Putting the Service-Profit Chain to Work," *Harvard Business Review* (March-April 1994): 173.

13. Peters and Austin, *A Passion for Excellence,* 77.

7

Love Your Coworker As Yourself

A ll the employees at Jones & Associates rushed through the door by 7:50 A.M. to get a jump on their day—and their boss. Frank would be arriving promptly at 8 A.M., the only time during normal working hours he was sure to be in the office.

Steve noticed the piles of materials stacked in each of their "in" baskets. "He's been staying up late again," grumbled the associate consultant. Steve's basket contained a bulging client folder for a project he knew nothing about. Frank had scribbled a brief note, saying he hadn't had time to get to this, so Steve needed to drop everything to finish the contracted work. As usual, the project was due tomorrow.

Laurie glanced over and saw Steve shaking his head, so she hurried over to check her own basket. It contained a copy of a major proposal she had submitted to Frank several days ago. The draft had been thoroughly slashed up with red ink from her boss' correction pen. Attached with a paper clip was a curt note simply saying, "Try again."

Beverly noticed the familiar cassette tape from Frank's dictation machine waiting in her box. She grabbed the tape and hurried back to her desk. Frank always dictated at least one "urgent" letter each night, expecting to see it waiting on his desk ready to sign the next morning.

Frank Jones rushed through the outer door, stopping briefly at the table in the reception waiting area to scoop up the morning newspaper. "Mornin', where's the McPherson letter?" he asked

Beverly as he glided by, distracted by the front-page headlines.

"Just finished typing it. The printer should have it cranked out in a few minutes."

Frank stopped the march to his office and looked up from his paper. "A few minutes? It shouldn't take that long to print one lousy letter."

"No, it shouldn't," replied Beverly in her best imitation of a calm voice. "But if you recall, I warned you last month that we would need to replace my computer when you purchased that word processing program upgrade. This old thing is just not fast enough."

Frank just shrugged. "Well, is the coffee ready yet?"

Beverly glared at him, then turned her attention back to the computer screen.

Both Steve and Laurie looked up, first acknowledging Frank's arrival and then spying that the other had noticed too. It would be a race to Frank's door since he rarely had time to address more than one problem per morning.

Laurie won the race, but the finish line was being closed in her face. "Sorry, you two," said Frank, peeking through the crack in the door. "Gotta big client presentation coming up in an hour. Can't you help each other with your problems?"

"I'm too busy with my own problems to help her out too," Steve protested. The door shut and the two underlings returned to their desks.

How many of us would get excited at the prospect of working for such a firm? Well, those of us who are positive thinkers might point out its great potential for ministry. Otherwise, the list of reasons for joining this company could easily fit on the back of a business card—in large print.

Truth is, we'd all like to work in a place where people honestly care for one another. Where employees are viewed as human beings, not "production units" or "resources." Where the work can be fun and the rewards generous but fair. Where the worker can feel proud of the company's products or services, knowing that they represent the company's best effort to meet customer needs. Where managers lead by example and act as cheerleaders, not traffic cops or drill sergeants.

> **Truth is, we'd all like to work in a place where people honestly care for one another.**

Unfortunately, few workplaces match up to that ideal. Yet, as Christians, the world's salt and light, we have the responsibility to do everything possible to bring about a caring work environment and avoid the "Frank Jones" syndrome. A good start to finding biblical support for our actions is to examine Christ's answer to the request to name the greatest commandment:

> "The most important one," answered Jesus, "is this: 'Hear, O Israel, the Lord our God, the Lord is one. Love the Lord your God with all your heart and with all your soul and with all your mind and with all your strength.' The second is this: 'Love your neighbor as yourself.' There is no commandment greater than these" (Mark 12:29-31).

Who is our neighbor, then? For Christians in the marketplace, the "neighbors" we see the most are generally the people with whom we work. On a busy workday, I may find myself face to face with as many as 100 different people. That is more neighbors than I've ever met in my suburban neighborhood.

The Servant Coworker

The concept of being a servant presented in the last chapter fits in well with loving your neighbor. Being Christ to customers and being Christ to coworkers requires many of the same attributes, such as caring, listening, and keeping their trust.

For companies, caring for customers and caring for employees are not only related tasks, but also seem to have a cause-and-effect relationship. Taking care of workers seems to be necessary for a company to take good care of customers. Paul Hawken, cofounder of the Smith & Hawken gardening catalog company, describes how he balanced worker and customer needs:

> When we did get around to writing down our service guidelines we were surprised by them. They almost say more about our attitude toward ourselves than toward our customers. The customer comes first? Not really. The employees come first. Employees' attitudes toward customers reflect their

treatment by their employers. They cannot serve unless served. There's no way to instill a positive customer service ethic before you embody a positive employee ethic. Responsiveness in, responsiveness out. [1]

On the other hand, having a company focus on serving customers also helps develop a good working environment. Peters and Waterman assert that "those companies that emphasize quality, reliability, and service have chosen the *only* area where it is readily possible to generate excitement in the average down-the-line employee. They give people pride in what they do. They make it possible to love the product." [2]

Serving As Jesus Would

Loving your neighbor as yourself cuts to the heart of a Christian's ministry on earth. It involves attempting to love others the way God loves us. Or, better yet, letting God's love flow through us to enrich the lives of others.

For me, the love-thy-neighbor concept has been easy to understand but hard to apply with consistency and regularity. Love is such an all-encompassing term, particularly in our society where it can be used to describe both Christ's sacrificial death and a satisfying pepperoni pizza.

One way to make the command more practical is to think of ourselves as Christ's representatives here on earth, part of His church, the body of Christ. If Christ dwells within us and we allow His love to flow through us, then we can spend our workday asking the challenging question made famous in the Charles Sheldon novel, *In His Steps*: "What would Jesus do?"

Sheldon's characters turned their town upside down by applying that question to their lives. Imagine asking ourselves that question in our daily interactions with others. How would Jesus treat His secretary? How would Jesus respond to outstanding employees? To lazy employees or those with obsolete skills?

These are tough questions to ask ourselves, partly because they require taking an up-close look at the flawless character of Jesus, whose loving responses to life's situations are always going to make our own responses look shoddy. Also, the Bible does not always provide simple, pat answers that cover every decision or action. To become more Christlike businesspeople, we must certainly study the Bible, and we must also spend time in reflection and prayer.

What would Jesus do if He worked in today's chaotic marketplace? How would He love His neighbor in the next cubicle or down the hall? As I've wrestled with those questions, I've discovered some answers.

1. Jesus would treat all workers with respect and as equals, regardless of their position in the company. To respect people is to consider them worthy of high regard or esteem, according to the dictionary. How many of us desire that kind of treatment? Part of loving our neighbor as ourself is treating another in a way we'd like to be treated—even when the organizational hierarchy might tempt us to "pull rank."

Christ's ministry on earth sought to counter the natural human tendency to give more respect to those of higher rank and status. His disciples were hardly the elite of their day. And He spent most of His time ministering to the sick and needy. Also, the church Jesus built recognizes the importance of each individual member. Scripture refers to the church as the body of Christ, meaning its members have different functions that together make the body function effectively. In 1 Corinthians 12:21-26, Paul notes that parts deemed less important by human standards are given special attention in Christ's church:

> The eye cannot say to the hand, "I don't need you!" And the head cannot say to the feet, "I don't need you!" On the contrary, those parts of the body that seem to be weaker are indispensable, and the parts that we think are less honorable we treat with special honor. And the parts that are unpresentable are treated with special modesty, while our presentable parts need no special treatment. But God has combined the members of the body and has given greater honor to the parts that lacked it, so that there should be no division in the body, but that its parts should have equal concern for each other. If one part suffers, every part suffers with it; if one part is honored, every part rejoices with it.

Love Your Coworker As Yourself

What a beautiful vision for the church—or any organization! Imagine if special attention were given to those toiling in the trenches: awards, mention in the internal newsletter, parking spots nearest the entrance, involvement in major company decisions. Who wouldn't want to work in an environment without division, without favoritism, and where individual successes are greeted with joy, not envy? If He were in the marketplace today, I'm certain that Jesus would try to develop a workplace like that.

Creating that sort of internal culture is a tall order for companies stricken with rigid hierarchies, widening pay discrepancies, and a constantly changing employee mix (via turnover and frequent cycles of layoffs). Even a simple matter like mutual respect can be a rare commodity. I recall one manager who frequently complained to others about the department's two secretaries. She seemed to especially dislike the fact that, when she rushed in with a project, the secretaries had the nerve to make suggestions for improvement. Since they were "just secretaries," the manager viewed their actions as an act of insubordination. Never mind that these secretaries each averaged about 20 years of experience with the company, compared to this newly hired manager. Those in the department who had been there for some time generally treated these women as peers by listening to them and respecting them. By treating these secretaries as inferiors this manager caused their morale to fall and their frustration level to increase.

Some companies are beginning to see the value of treating all employees with respect. Back in the 1970s, Wayne Alderson, then vice president of operations for Pittron Steel, led a dramatic business turnaround with the simple discovery that all workers wanted to be valued. His "Value of the Person" concept contained three key ingredients: love, dignity, and respect. To successfully introduce the concept into an industry with a history of bitter labor disputes was revolutionary.

Quite a few companies, many run by Christians, adhere to the Value of the Person approach. One of those organizations is ParaBody Fitness, makers of strength-building equipment for those committed to a fitness lifestyle. According to cofounder and President Jerry Dettinger, a core principle of the business is that people are "treated with love, dignity, and respect at all times." He says that new employees notice something different about the company, learning from other employees that their leader is a Christian who strives to run his company according to biblical principles.

2. Jesus would get "personal" with those He worked with. I remember learning somewhere in my early business training that it was unwise for a manager to get too close to those he or she supervised. If one got too close, workers would lose respect for the boss or figure they could take liberties without fear of discipline.

Very early in my career, I set that teaching aside. How could I be a caring manager if I kept the people I'm supposed to care about at arm's length? Although I haven't been close to all the people I've supervised, several good friendships have developed over the years. And, to refute my business instruction, clearly the best employees I've had so far have been those with whom I have developed a strong personal relationship.

No leader got closer to his followers than Jesus. His was not a nine-to-five, strictly business relationship with His disciples. In fact, Jesus socialized so much with His lowly followers that His detractors labeled Him "a friend of tax collectors and 'sinners'"(Matt. 11:19).

> **That Christ spent most of His three-year public ministry getting very personal with the men selected to lead His church is of great significance for those who seek to emulate Him in the workplace.**

That Christ spent most of His three-year public ministry getting very personal with the men selected to lead His church is of great significance for those who seek to emulate Him in the workplace. Most executives are trained to be analytical and task oriented. People are reduced to abstract, quantifiable terms such as *labor, productivity,* and *human resources.* There's no room in a manager's massive executive planner to recognize frivolous events such as birthdays or employment anniversaries.

Some companies have realized that people are too important to treat as mere "human resources" from which to extract maximum output. Firms like Herman Miller and ServiceMaster changed the title of their Vice President of Human Resources/Personnel to "Vice President for People," an indicator of what they feel is truly important.

James Autry, magazine group president of the Meredith Corporation, believes that businesses should go further than simply providing a decent place to work. "We managers have the opportunity to lead and direct people in that ever more powerful bond of common enterprise, and at the same time to create a place of friendship, deep personal connections, and neighborhood." [3]

What Autry and other business leaders advocate is creating a sense of community in the workplace. Why? Two reasons. First, work is where most people spend the bulk of their days. Also, other forms of community—families, neighborhoods, churches—apply to fewer in our culture today than in years past.

In corporations that attempt to create an environment where people care deeply for one another, wonderful things can happen. When a woman at ParaBody Fitness came down with cancer, two other employees approached the president with a desire to support her. They threw a barbeque party for their fellow employee, complete with a raffle, that raised $15,000. "It was a very moving experience," said Dettinger.

3. Jesus would pray for His coworkers and their needs. It didn't take me very long to come up with this point. The Gospels record frequent times when Jesus prayed, so few can doubt that He would pray if He worked in our organization today.

> **As simple as the act of prayer appears, this may be the most potent way we can be like Jesus in the marketplace.**

As simple as the act of prayer appears, this may be the most potent way we can be like Jesus in the marketplace. If we truly desire to make business our ministry, then praying for those who work alongside us is essential. For if we are not regularly praying for our coworkers, how do we expect God to use us to minister to them?

If you are at all like me, this concept can be humbling. When work gets frantic and the deadlines stack up, the extra hours at the office often crowd out time normally spent in prayer. According to Dick Eastman, founder of Change the World Ministries, this will seriously hinder our ability to minister to the needs of others:

No matter our position in life or natural abilities, to be mightily used of God we must first understand a fundamental principle of spiritual power. What we do for the Lord is entirely dependent upon what we are in the Lord. Further, what we are in the Lord wholly depends upon what we receive from the Lord. And what we receive from the Lord is directly proportional to the time we spend alone with the Lord in prayer. To spend little time with Jesus is to accomplish little in Jesus.[4]

How do we begin to accomplish something for Jesus where we work? A worthy start would be to make a list of those with whom you work closely and then pray for them all at least once a week. If you put their names on an index card, you can carry it with you and pray for them each and every work- day.

Another good prayer idea is to gather together with other Christians. The Christian Business Men's Committee I attend has a weekly prayer breakfast, where I marvel at seeing my prayer requests being offered up simultaneously by pairs of men bowing before God. Members of my church meet early every Thursday morning to pray through a list of unsaved people that currently runs sixteen pages.

In some companies, Christians get together regularly to pray for coworkers in need. William Walton, Sr., cofounder of Holiday Inns, Inc., used to meet every Wednesday morning with eighty top managers for coffee and devotionals, using the time to pray for employees in crisis or need. At Cray Research, longtime innovators in computer technology, I visited a small group of workers who met over lunch for prayer and support, using electronic mail to notify participants of future meetings.

Another way to make prayer more effective relates back to getting personal with our fellow laborer. It's hard to pray in any detail for strangers. We don't know their hopes, hurts, and struggles—or even if they need salvation. The more meaningful interaction we have with people, the more likely we are to learn of specific prayer requests.

In some circumstances, letting the other person know you're praying for him or her can be a gesture of caring. One of Kathy's coworkers had long desired a career change and was being considered for a job well-suited to her. Our small group cell from church prayed for that situation and, when she landed the job, she gave credit to God and those prayers.

When we pray for those we spend time with from 8-to-5 each day, we need to be prepared to be a part of God's answer. Our prayer time may become more than simply laying requests before God; He may empower us by the Holy Spirit to minister to our coworkers in tangible ways.

One morning, during a week I was hopelessly behind with projects, I entered my office to find a memo slipped under the door. The daughter of one of our secretaries had just been killed in a head-on collision with a truck. My natural reaction was to pray for the victim and her family—and leave it at that. I've done it before. This time, God nudged me away from my projects to spend time with two women in the department who had also lost immediate family members during the past two years (one in an almost identical circumstance). After shedding their tears, they decided to help by bringing trays of food to the house so that no one in the grieving family would have to worry about cooking. They asked me to go with them, more for support than for practical reasons. God had turned my prayers into a very small but tangible assignment.

We imitate Christ, therefore, when we lift up workplace requests to the Father. Prayer, however, is by no means the sum total of our business ministry. It is but a launching pad for God to use us as instruments for good in the marketplace.

4. Jesus would publicly recognize the hard work and achievements of His coworkers. During Christ's ministry on earth, He was forever pointing out and praising acts of faith. When the humble centurion asked Jesus to heal his servant in Matthew 8, he asked only for the healer's word, since he felt he didn't "deserve to have You come under my roof."

Christ was quick to praise this act in front of His followers, saying, "I tell you the truth, I have not found anyone in Israel with such great faith" (Matt. 8:10).

How rare such praise is. One study of families (cited at a sales workshop I attended) showed that in an average family, children are criticized or corrected about five times more than they are praised. At most job sites, that particular ratio still seems to hold true.

Supervisors act more like traffic cops, waiting in the wings for someone to mess up. Other workers act more like wild bucks protecting their turf than as part of a cohesive team.

Jesus had a better way. Despite training disciples with raw, untested abilities, Christ was quick to praise a right response, constantly modeled proper behavior, and corrected without demeaning the individual. A Christian in today's business world could make quite an impact imitating those three traits.

One way of countering the impulse to be merely a rule enforcer is to practice its antithesis: spend time being a cheerleader. Try to "catch" people doing something right (instead of wrong) and praise them for it. You may not feel natural doing this at first, but the startled and delighted responses of those you praise will make your effort seem worthwhile.

Combining praise with a reward can really send morale skyrocketing. One day at Hewlett-Packard, an engineer came to his manager with news that he had solved a long-standing problem. The manager searched his desk for something to accompany his praise and proudly awarded his employee a banana from his lunch. That act gave birth to the prestigious Golden Banana Award the company gives to reward especially inventive employees.

> **Despite training disciples with raw, untested abilities, Christ was quick to praise a right response, constantly modeled proper behavior, and corrected without demeaning the individual.**

Sometimes absurdly simple rewards like a banana can cause great changes in behavior. When I teach evening marketing classes, I have each student present his or her marketing plan orally with "real world" time limits of five to ten minutes. I was frustrated at how frequently these limits were exceeded, with students droning on in exhaustive detail for up to half an hour. When one student gave a superb presentation in exactly five minutes, I rushed over to my backpack and awarded her a bag of mixed nuts. Nearly half the students who followed her that night also met the time limit—a first. The next time I taught, I announced the award for well-prepared, timely presentations in advance. Not a single student went over the maximum time limit.

Recognition and rewards mustn't always relate to day-to-day achievements. At Herman Miller, Inc., employees who have served the company for 20 years or more have their names inscribed around the base of a sculpture depicting an American Indian water-carrier, along with this message:

> The tribal watercarrier in this corporation is a symbol of the essential nature of all jobs, our interdependence, the identity of ownership and participation, the servanthood of leadership, the authenticity of each individual. [5]

Celebrations don't need to be related to work happenings either. At happy work sites, people look for excuses to throw a party. Birthdays, anniversaries, weddings, and new babies are all good reasons for people to get together for food and presents. One event that became tradition in our department at HealthEast is the Stress Relief Seminar. Nearly every summer, we'd pick an afternoon to take off early and gather at a pool or lake to relax, have water fights, and consume lots of junk food. It's a simple recognition of the need to counter the effects of a year filled with long hours and impossible deadlines.

5. *Jesus would encourage His fellow workers to develop themselves.* I've heard that the mark of a great leader is the ability to raise up others to lead in the future. On that account, Christ would measure up as the greatest leader in history. He took a brash fisherman named Peter and created a courageous leader for His new church. Matthew, the tax collector-turned-apostle, was a highly visible witness to the life-changing properties of Christianity, applying his fondness for detail to writing a Gospel depicting all he had seen and heard. James and John, the sons of Zebedee, were filled with great ambition, which Jesus channeled toward God instead of selfishness. James was the first apostle to be martyred, while John was credited as a pillar of the church and a New Testament writer.

Although Christ had authority over His disciples, He did not manage them in the way we traditionally view employer-employee relationships. He led by example and through ongoing teaching and training. He knew that simply telling His followers what to do and think would not adequately prepare them to carry on God's work when He was not physically present.

In the marketplace, we need to realize that the traditional way of managing people—telling them what to do, looking for mistakes, drafting up notebooks full of rules and policies, refusing to delegate important matters—does not help people develop to their fullest and saps all the motivation from their beings. Notice I refer to managing as sapping worker motivation, implying that every person carries some kind of motivation to work each day. The key for effective managers is to provide a work situation where each person's passion and energy are allowed to be released.

Accomplishing this is no easy task. It involves significant training, both formal and informal, to ensure that each employee can perform his or her task with great skill, flair, and pride. Managers must especially be on the lookout for each person's unique talents and passions, finding ways to apply them somewhere in the job or company. By discovering and germinating those seeds of greatness, we perform a wonderful service to our organization and the employees themselves.

During the writing of this book, my role at HealthEast changed from being Director of Marketing for a division of the firm to Corporate Sales Administrator. This was a new position, so I had endless possibilities on how to proceed. It is no coincidence that one of the first tangible projects I implemented happened to be something I personally wanted to do. An informal monthly sales newsletter called *Sales Stuff* was not something the organization said they needed. Although the newsletter addresses a number of stated communication and training needs, I could meet them through other methods. This approach, however, makes the best use of my interests and abilities, giving the organization a communication vehicle proudly produced with love. It also gives me a fun break from the more stressful aspects of my new position.

Helping employees to be all they can be is a significant ministry that can dramatically change the lives of individuals and energize entire companies. Unfortunately, too few firms place a high priority on bringing people along. ServiceMaster does. The company's two main end goals, according to President and Chief Executive Officer C. William Pollard, are to "honor God in all we do" and "to help people develop." [6] Imagine how great work would be if all organizations adopted and fulfilled those goals!

Love Your Coworker As Yourself

Think about It

❑ How much time per month do you spend socially with your coworkers? How much do you know about your coworkers' personal lives?

❑ In what specific ways can you love your coworkers more—especially those with whom you work most closely?

❑ If Jesus had your job, how would He treat your coworkers? List specifics.

❑ How often do you pray for your coworkers?

Notes

1. Paul Hawken, *Growing a Business* (New York: Simon and Schuster, 1987), 197.

2. Thomas J. Peters and Robert H. Waterman, Jr., *In Search of Excellence* (New York: Warner Books, 1982), 180.

3. James A. Autry, *Love & Profit* (New York: William Morrow and Company, Inc., 1991), 145.

4. Dick Eastman, *The Hour That Changes the World* (Grand Rapids: Baker Book House, 1978), 14.

5. Max DePree, *Leadership Jazz* (New York: Dell Publishing, 1992), 65.

6. Robert J. Tamasy, "Ethics and the Fortune 500: A CEO's Perspective," in *The Complete Christian Businessman*, ed. Robert J. Tamasy (Brentwood, Tenn.: Wolgemuth & Hyatt, Publishers, Inc., 1991), 26.

8

Work with Integrity
and Honesty

··

Terms such as *integrity* and *honesty* get tossed around frequently, both in secular and Christian circles. How does a Christian live with integrity and honesty each day in a bottom-line business world? To better identify the issues, let's look at a morning in the life of a businessman I'll call Bob.

It is a quarter after nine when Bob pulls his company car into its reserved spot near the front door. Bob always has trouble pulling himself away from morning breakfast Bible studies because of all the great Christian fellowship. Some weeks he attends three or four such meetings, causing the work to pile up on his desk.

First on his agenda this morning is a meeting with Steve in human resources. Bob has two decisions to approve: the issuance of bonus checks to managers for last fiscal year's record performance and laying off twenty employees. That last decision is difficult to make, especially since Bob convinced employees that last year's wage concessions would help preserve their jobs. However, he can't see any way of continuing the firm's stellar financial performance without pinching back labor costs.

After the meeting, Bob finds a fax on his desk from an out-of-state friend. It is an article on bathroom remodeling, something Bob mentioned he was considering during their last telephone conversation. He makes a photocopy of the article for an interested colleague, then picks up the phone to thank his friend for the thoughtful gesture.

Finally, Bob receives a phone call from a charitable foundation looking for a corporate contribution. This group was well-known for supporting abortion rights organizations, so he politely tells the caller that money is tight and he cannot contribute.

How many challenges to Bob's integrity could you find in this story? And how did Bob rise to the occasion?

Some of the challenges Bob faced were easy to spot. The contribution to the foundation was even obvious to Bob, although he was not completely honest in his reason for saying no. Also, the situation with the simultaneous bonuses and layoffs is fertile ground for integrity questions. Either way Bob tries to tighten the company belt here creates a problem of broken promises. If he goes through with the layoffs, he breaks a labor promise. If he doesn't pay bonuses to managers who worked to earn them, he breaks another promise.

Other integrity compromises are little things that, in the long run, aren't so little. Regularly missing work time—even for the best of reasons—robs the company of some of Bob's talents. Also, using company equipment (copier, fax machine, long-distance phone service) for personal needs is dishonest and diverts money from other business purposes. Even the reserved parking space and the company car may create integrity problems, particularly for workers who have to park farther away and walk past the empty space each morning.

Although I think we all would aspire for a better track record than Bob's, the constant testing of his integrity is typical of what many of us in the marketplace encounter every day. With the flood of news reports about business and political leaders facing criminal charges or forced resignations, it is clear that honesty and integrity are two traits in short supply.

Honesty and Integrity Defined

What do these two terms mean and how are they related? Most people would define honesty this way: telling the truth, being sincere, conduct that is straightforward and fair. Defining integrity, on the other hand, is much like how I would describe my taste in art: I know what I like and don't like when I see it.

I've tried to define integrity with more precision. Basically, integrity is adherance to a set of righteous values. Honesty is certainly one of those values, as is being trustworthy, faithful, genuine, consistent, fair, and compassionate. Thus, in today's turbulent sea of moral upheaval, people of integrity are like a lighthouse on solid ground. You can depend on them and look to them for guidance.

> **Thus, in today's turbulent sea of moral upheaval, people of integrity are like a lighthouse on solid ground.**

Doug Sherman and William Hendricks, in their book, *Keeping Your Ethical Edge Sharp*, point out that integrity goes beyond being a good example for others:

> "Integrity has to do with our behavior when no one is watching—no one, that is, except God. When we're out making sales calls, when we're alone in our office, when we're making deliveries, when we're at a convention—when we're all alone, do we still work as if the boss were right there next to us? We should, because our ultimate Boss is! [1]

This thought is related to that of Colossians 3:22-24, where slaves are instructed to obey their earthly masters "not only when their eye is on you and to win their favor, but with sincerity of heart and reverence for the Lord." Since the passage also says it is the Lord Christ who is the ultimate master or boss, there should be no difference between a Christian's public and private conduct. For the man or woman of integrity, the One who matters most is always watching over our work.

God is very concerned about the honesty and integrity present in our work performance. "The LORD detests lying lips, but He delights in men who are truthful," states Proverbs 12:22. In Deuteronomy 25:13-16, God lays down the law against having differing weights and measures—an ancient equivalent of today's deceptive tactics to squeeze out an extra buck, such as inflated personal expense reports and bogus tax deductions. The LORD "detests anyone who does these things, anyone who deals dishonestly."

Becoming a person of integrity is also important, according to Proverbs 10:9, because integrity allows us to "walk securely," unlike those who choose the crooked path and will ultimately be found out.

In the Old Testament, God directly labeled two men as having integrity: Job (Job 2:3) and David (1 Kings 9:4). Even though neither man was perfect, studying their lives can provide great insight. Both maintained their integrity under extreme circumstances. Job faced every tragedy known to man, and David was constantly on the run from King Saul, who was trying to kill him.

Integrity's Value to Work

Besides being an important aspect of Christian character, integrity is considered by many to be the most important trait for business leaders today. Max DePree of Herman Miller, Inc. calls integrity the "linchpin of leadership,"[2] while Lawrence Miller, author of *American Spirit: Visions of a New Corporate Culture*, believes that integrity must be the "most certain" of the qualities of the new kind of leader:

> Leadership requires followship and following is an act of trust, faith in the course of the leader, and that faith can be generated only if leaders act with integrity.... The person or organization that has integrity can be trusted. From trust comes security, the individual's knowledge of how the world around will respond to his actions. There can be no leadership without integrity. [3]

Integrity and honesty have been good qualities to possess throughout history, according to Tom Peters. In the more chaotic future, however, he believes these traits become "must-do" items because employees will require an atmosphere of trust to do what businesses need in order to survive. "If a promise (even a minor one) is not kept, if ethics are compromised, and if management behaves inconsistently, then the strategies necessary to survival today simply can't be executed." [4]

Many of the problems in business, especially employee problems, can be traced to issues of integrity. Labor unions did not come about out of a sense of greed, but because workers did not trust management to provide safe working conditions and tolerable wages. Most businesses required outside pressure to treat workers right, which still breeds adversity between labor and management in many industries.

Adversity and lack of trust are costly to business, both directly and indirectly. Although employee theft is a problem for many businesses, it seems most rampant in situations where employees felt the company "owed" them something. After high school, I worked part-time for a local discount retailer where few employees made much beyond minimum wage. I remember watching stock clerks open large cardboard boxes of bagged candy bars, "accidentally" slashing their knives too deeply, causing a number of bags to be ripped open. These damaged goods would have to return to the stockroom, where the clerks could eat them during break. I recall being too uneasy about the practice to accept their invitation to feast on the spoils, yet not brave enough to help bring the theft to an end.

> **The damage that results from breaches of integrity and honesty is often difficult to reverse.**

In more recent years, an expensive camera disappeared from our department during a rash of employee layoffs. I guess someone felt the severance package needed supplementing.

The damage that results from breaches of integrity and honesty is often difficult to reverse. Entrepreneurial expert Paul Hawken believes that customers and employees give each new business the benefit of the doubt, but it's often a one-time chance:

> If you're starting out in business you have a grace that you can always keep. If you start with quality and the truth you'll never have to stop. There will be no reason to. But once you stop telling customers the truth—or don't tell the truth from the beginning—you'll find it's difficult to start later. The value of honesty, like virginity, lies in its irreplaceability. I'm not talking about image, either. I am talking about what's genuine. You become what you say, and what you say becomes you. [5]

How employees perceive what their employer says is critical to the building of integrity and trust. A company once hired a manager who came aboard thinking he would be embarking on a large-scale business project. He began setting up for his task with great energy and enthusiasm. Unfortunately, money for the project was nowhere near being approved when he was hired. In fact, budgets were going to be lean for the coming fiscal year, which meant that funds for new projects would be as likely as flowers during a Minnesota winter.

As it turned out, the great campaign that so excited this new manager didn't materialize during his first or even his second year of employment. I don't know if this employee was actually lied to, but he obviously felt misled. The company lost its integrity in his eyes—a loss that's hard to measure on the bottom line. After all, who can add up the cost of lost enthusiasm and energy?

Integrity's Impact on Our Witness

For Christians, the issues of integrity and honesty present both a great opportunity and a substantial risk. The opportunity is perhaps at a level never before seen in our lifetime. For the more evil grows in the marketplace, the more Christians of integrity will stand out. The effect we can have is best illustrated by a photocopy of an advertisement attached to my filing cabinet at work. The headline reads, "The Best Reason for Advertising in a Recession." The artwork shows a line of bare trees, except for one lush tree with leaves. When the world's moral base is bare and lifeless, the woman or man of integrity will stand out as a work of beauty.

So what's the risk? Well, once that lone, green tree gets the attention of others, people continue to watch it closely to see if it's for real. Even Christ's rivals, the Pharisees, publicly acknowledged His integrity (Matthew 22:16; Mark 12:14), but that did not stop them from watching, testing, and questioning Jesus, hoping they could find some inconsistency.

Visible Christians in business are like Jesus in that others watch our activities very carefully. And should we ever dismiss our importance in the scheme of things, Doug Sherman of Career Impact Ministries issues a stern reminder:

Whatever efforts ministries and missions exert through their programs will have little effect if people don't see genuine Christianity at work. All the sermons, television shows, pamphlets, and crusades in the world are unlikely to overcome the deep skepticism people feel once they see a person who claims to know Christ compromise his integrity—especially if he does so repeatedly and unashamedly. What this boils down to, then, is *your* integrity before a watching world. [6]

What a humbling thought! To think that my actions may impact someone's decision to embrace Christ or dismiss Him is unnerving. For, unlike Christ, I still sin, offering ammunition to those who'd like to label Christians as hypocrites. Although Christ will forgive my sins when I confess and repent, the consequences of my actions in the minds of those who witness them will remain.

However, our reaction to sin or to situations that challenge our integrity can have a positive impact. As I mentioned in an earlier chapter, Jim Bever has twice faced large financial challenges in his landscaping business. Each time the easiest course of action would have been to declare bankruptcy, pay his debtors a fraction of what he owed, and start over. Imagine how his ability to be a witness for Christ would have been hampered with his suppliers had they not been paid.

Instead, Jim stayed in business and slowly paid off each debt. Although Jim's decision to dig himself out of debt probably won him little applause—because vendors dislike being paid late—he avoided action which would have created long-term damage to his substantial evangelism efforts.

We need to understand, therefore, that our integrity can serve either as an evangelistic lighthouse or a land mine, depending on our actions. Acts showing Christ's character will serve as a beacon to guide others to the Lord. When we stumble into sin, however, our mistakes cause damage similar to a triggered land mine, hurting ourselves, our witness, and possibly others close to us.

How to Develop Integrity in the Workplace

How do we become a lighthouse of integrity that burns brighter and brighter with each passing year? Here are four things to do that will help.

1. Tell the truth in all circumstances. This is a very basic and obvious point, but most people violate this without even realizing it. For instance, little white lies seem to make the day go by easier. Tell the boss the plan looks great, exaggerate the interruptions that kept you from turning in the project on time, respond positively to the waitress who inquires about your lukewarm lunch. Even talking behind someone's back violates truthfulness because we're usually saying something different from what we tell the person face-to-face.

Please realize that being honest isn't sharing every thought and opinion that comes to mind, regardless of who gets hurt. When a businessperson says, "let's be honest," a verbal bombshell usually follows. Sin is unavoidable when words are many, according to Proverbs 10:19. "But he who holds his tongue is wise."

Some industries have an image for wording that shades the truth. A friend of mine was a salesperson for an auto dealership for many years, despite being at odds with management's approach. He knew the best long-term strategy was to treat customers right and be honest with them—and he had the sales record to back it up. During tight financial times, however, management pressured its sales staff to do or say anything to make each customer walk off the lot with a new vehicle. Sales managers would even intercept his customers on their way out to see if they could force a deal. Management felt, at one point, it had to change the tactics of this top salesperson because his success might cause other, younger sales staffers to abandon company tactics.

My friend endured this conflict without resorting to the deceptive deal-making that gives car salespeople their slick, plaid-jacket reputation. Eventually he started up a business of his own as an auto broker and, with his reputation for honesty, many long-time customers continued to trust him with their vehicle purchases.

2. Take nothing extra from your employer or customers. In business, employees have almost limitless opportunities to steal from their employers in many, tiny increments. Using the copier or fax machine for personal business, taking product "samples" home, and falsely calling in sick are all small thefts but, in large firms, they can add up to thousands or even millions of dollars.

Years ago, I received telephone messages at work from a close, out-of-town friend. Without thinking, I would pick up the phone in my office and dial him up, usually just leaving a message on his voice mail. Initially, I rationalized it as an executive perk. Besides, it only added up to a few dollars.

God quickly convinced me through His Word that I was wrong. In biblical times, a common "little theft" was to use two different sets of weights and measures in the marketplace; a generous set to use when purchasing something and a skimpy set for when someone bought from you. The differences had to be slight, otherwise the other party would notice. The dishonest gain would take many transactions to amount to much. Yet God singles out this practice for condemnation several times in the Old Testament, including Leviticus 19:35-36, Deuteronomy 25:13-16, and Proverbs 20:10, 23.

Now I always have a long-distance calling card with me at work, which only takes a few seconds longer to use when I make calls on my lunch hour.

If you have direct dealings with customers, opportunities to mislead or cheat them abound. One company got in serious legal trouble and angered millions of parents by selling colored water as apple juice. In another instance, a parking lot attendent skimmed a few extra bucks by making "math errors" when giving out change.

The important thing to remember is there is no theft too small in God's eyes.

3. Only make promises you can be certain to keep. When a boss, employee, spouse, or pastor asks you to do something, the first reaction (if the request is reasonable) is usually to say yes. If the requests come in too quickly, you get overwhelmed, finally realizing that you have committed to more than you can complete.

Much of the hectic busyness in each of our lives comes from cramming too many commitments into the calendar. Sometimes, when the load gets too heavy, we delay or renege on something we promised to do. When we fail to complete our commitments, our standing as a reliable worker of integrity is questioned by those we have let down. Many years later, I still remember the disappointed tone in my associate pastor's voice after I told him I no longer had the time to edit the church's newsletter for singles after just one very successful issue.

All commitments should be taken very seriously because their fulfillment is a godly act. The Old Testament is filled with God's promises to Israel, with Psalm 145:13 declaring "the LORD is faithful to all His promises."

We should seek to emulate that complete faithfulness, for even small broken promises undermine trust and integrity. Let's say you take your car into the repair shop on Monday, and the mechanic tells you it will be ready to pick up on Wednesday. When Wednesday comes, you call and are told it will take longer. Please call back on Friday.

It's irritating when that happens, isn't it? If this happens again, will you ever believe your mechanic's promises? Wouldn't you have felt better if he had promised it on Friday in the first place? Wouldn't you feel even better if he had finished the work a day before he had promised?

A wise approach to making commitments is to be slow to give your word and conservative in what you promise to do— whether that promise is to your employer, employees, or customers. If possible, don't say yes right away; allow yourself time to check your schedule, think, and pray about it. For instance, if you esti-

> **When we fail to complete our commitments, our standing as a reliable worker of integrity is questioned by those we have let down.**

mate a project will take a week to complete if everything goes right, it is not wise to commit to that because, most weeks, something does go wrong. Since we cannot know all that tomorrow may bring, we need to anticipate the unexpected in order to have some flexibility in meeting our commitments.

Sometimes it is difficult to anticipate everything. When St. John's Hospital built a new hospital in the suburbs, it wanted to reassure those who used their Eastside facility—located near downtown—of their continued commitment to the hospital. As work on the suburban facility began, ads ran for the city hospital with the headline, "St. John's Eastside Is Here to Stay." When St. John's Northeast opened, its full-page newspaper advertisements always included a matching ad for St. John's Eastside on the facing page.

Then the unforeseen happened: a joint venture with other hospital companies in the city left the new organization with too many hospitals ringing the downtown area. Plans to close St. John's Eastside were announced two years after the opening of the new suburban hospital. Some of those who lived near Eastside remembered the advertising campaign and were upset at the news.

4. Treat others with respect and appreciation. You've probably heard the saying: if you want people to act like adults, treat them like adults. It sounds so simple, yet many managers and businesses act as if their employees were unruly fifth-graders. Strict dress codes, massive policy manuals, surveillance cameras, and sharing company information on a "need-to-know" basis hardly makes people feel like responsible adults.

For example, strict (and often silly) rules create an atmosphere of dishonesty because nearly everyone breaks them. And sometimes following the rules costs the company more money than breaking them. Once, a department manager got approval in the capital budget to replace some ancient, broken-down office furniture. She was careful to make good use of the money, selecting items that were functional and modest.

A week or so later, she was informed that the desks were unallowable as a capital item because, when the vendor discount was subtracted, each desk cost a little less than the $500 minimum rule for capital purchases. She would either have to pay for them out of her operating budget (where no money was available) or order more expensive desks. Since this rule was strictly enforced, she felt her only choice was to order more expensive desks.

Tom Peters urges organizations to eliminate bureaucracy and demeaning rules, which tend to invite game playing and slow down those trying to take positive action. He believes that efforts to eliminate Mickey Mouse rules in business are important "enhancers of integrity." [7]

Another practice that impacts integrity is the way an organization treats those they lay off. In many large corporations, executives must leave the day they are terminated, cleaning out their desks under the watchful eye of an escort, who is there to ensure that important company property stays and that the ex-employee leaves. The only time I've seen this attempted, scores of fellow employees complained and had the practice eliminated, stating that the action was an unneeded slap in the face to those who had been loyal, dedicated managers just one day earlier.

Besides eliminating rules and practices that show disrespect for workers, another way of enhancing integrity involves making people feel appreciated. According to Kenneth Blanchard and Norman Vincent Peale, appreciated employees will help management create a business with integrity:

> If people feel appreciated...they are more likely to resist the temptation to act unethically. If they are proud of their company and what it represents, people will fight to maintain integrity in the organization. [8]

Integrity Is Not Created Overnight

As I began writing this chapter, nearly every dishonest and sinful act of my life burst into my mind like a flood. I thought, how could I in my imperfection ever be considered a person of integrity?

If you too feel that your shortcomings might disqualify you, don't worry. For everyone but God, integrity is not a destination to be reached but rather a lifelong journey. According to Sherman and Hendricks, Christians seeking to do right possess what is called progressive integrity:

> They realize that biblical integrity is not natural; it takes focused attention. They have learned that the scope of biblical integrity is broader than a few principles easily mastered. They know that the human heart is capable of rationalizing almost anything and have cultivated a healthy mistrust of themselves, allowing their actions to come under regular scrutiny of God's Word. They come to the Scriptures with great humility, knowing that each pass at a scriptural principle could bring new application and insight. Finally, they realize that God is gracious enough to us [sic] to not reveal [sic] *all* the sin in our life at once, choosing to progressively reveal areas in our life that He wants to conquer. Thus, honesty is a path we are on, not a point we achieve. [9]

Developing integrity is a little like cleaning up broken glass. First, you clear away the biggest and most obvious pieces. Then you begin to notice all the tiny chips and slivers. As you carefully sweep away all but the smallest specks, it may seem as if you'll never end up with a clean surface. Yet, most people you meet are more likely to notice the nice clean-up job than the slivers you missed, seeing you as a person of integrity. (Also, in God's eyes, His forgiveness gives us a clean slate). Plus, as you continue to notice and clean up the tiny bits of sin in your life, you'll be sure to notice and be on guard against the big stuff.

> **For everyone but God, integrity is not a destination to be reached but rather a lifelong journey.**

According to Jerry Dettinger of ParaBody Fitness Equipment, it is the little stuff—the "little gray areas" in business—where the spiritual battle really lies. Once a salesperson brought in an unused airline ticket for Jerry to take for a business trip. This particular ticket had been issued in the salesperson's name and, according to its specifications, was not meant to be transferable.

All the CEO would have to do is show up at the airport with the ticket and "be" the salesperson for the flight—lots of people do it. Jerry, however, decided the right thing to do was "to play by the rules."

Playing by the rules and showing integrity in small matters is important for several reasons. First, as far as integrity and honesty are concerned, there are no "small matters." According to Tom Peters, small issues are sometimes the most important:

> Integrity may be about little things as much as or more than big ones. It's about executives taking friends, rather than customers, to sit in the company's box seats at the ballpark. It's about pushing salespeople at the end of a quarter to place orders, knowing that many will be canceled within the week—but that the cancellations will count in the next period for accounting purposes. These "minor" lapses set a tone of disrespect for people, products, systems, customers, distributors, and relationships that can readily become pervasive. That is, there is no such thing as a minor lapse in integrity. [10]

Also, how we react in small matters is important because it sets the tone for what we'll do in larger issues and temptations that will eventually come our way. Small sins can be habit- forming and make us a little more receptive to sins that are not so small. Finally, pleasing God in small things will open the way up for larger ministry opportunities. In the Parable of the Shrewd Manager found in Luke 16, Jesus instructs His disciples to be trustworthy with money and property so that they will be ready to handle increasingly greater responsibilities:

> Whoever can be trusted with very little can also be trusted with much, and whoever is dishonest with very little will also be dishonest with much. So if you have not been trustworthy in handling worldly wealth, who will trust you with true riches? And if you have not been trustworthy with someone else's property, who will give you property of your own? (Luke 16:10-12)

I feel it is important to be very watchful of our own behavior—even to the point of overkill—so we'll have the character we need to face the larger challenges of life. For example, after I decided I needed to use a long-distance calling card at work, I began seeing other behaviors I should change. Now, I try to keep track of the origin of every piece of paper, pen, or paper clip I use to ensure that nothing my employer purchased is used for my own personal business.

The Power of Perception

Ideally, all Christian workers would greatly develop in the areas of honesty and integrity, causing those working around us to notice our impeccable character and begin to search for its source. In the real world, however, Christians aren't perfect. And because there is so much sin in the world, sometimes our integrity will take a beating in the minds of our fellow workers, even when we haven't done anything wrong.

I faced such a situation one day during the year I wrote this book. I spent most of that day in my office on the computer, working on a newsletter and a variety of sales-related projects. When I emerged from my office late in the afternoon, another worker asked me how many pages I had written today. I asked for clarification and learned this person was inquiring about my book.

The question floored me. It had never occurred to me that others might think I was writing the book on company time. Although I sometimes spent lunch hours researching and outlining, not a single page of text was written from my office. Few people in the department knew such a task was impossible, given the incompatibility of my obsolete computer at home with my newer model at work. People saw me spending long hours in my office at the computer and assumed something else was going on.

Often our innocent actions will be misinterpreted, and there's little we can do about it. Sometimes, however, we can engage in activities that look wrong to others, even if we are not actually sinning. For example, to regularly come in to work an hour late and stay after an extra hour may be permissible in some firms—and a blessing to those who are not morning people. To those working regular hours, however, they will only witness the late arrival. We must sometimes judge the wisdom of our actions not only from our perspective, but also from the vantage point of others.

Earlier in my career, I felt I had discovered a perfect solution to making personal photocopies during work time. I frequently came across items I wanted to copy for my own use, yet I knew that copying on the company machine was stealing. My solution was to barter for the copies, not turning in mileage and other expenses in exchange for use of the machine. I only used the copier after normal business hours and, given the amount of expenses for which I didn't get reimbursed, the company was making money on the deal.

I thought I was being pretty smart until, one evening, another employee came in to use the machine. It was obvious I wasn't making copies for work. I remember trying to explain my arrangement to her, but I never finished because it sounded so lame. That was the last time I bartered for copies because I realized that the kind of integrity necessary to influence others must include behavior which is in all ways above question.

Integrity Is Contagious

As a Christian when you set high standards for integrity and honesty, you can feel as if you are going it alone in a business environment where the bottom line is often the only standard that counts. Yet, reaching for that standard will enable others to trust you and follow you with confidence. Then you won't be alone anymore.

When Lawrence Miller interviewed top business executives, he was impressed at how often these leaders were strongly influenced by mentors of high integrity:

> The best executives rather consistently point to powerful role models from whom they learned and to whom they feel they owe their success. When asked to describe these models or mentors, they almost invariably describe their character, their trustworthiness, their dedication. Their mentors took an interest in the development of their subordinates. They demonstrated true caring and concern. They took the time to help and assist and teach. They were not so preoccupied with immediate business that they failed to address the needs of their subordinates. And they, too, believed in something.... What higher achievement by a manager can there be than to leave to posterity others who have adopted his spirit of integrity and purpose?[11]

Never underestimate the powerful way God can use the "good guys" of this world. Imagine the potential impact of a large army of Christian men and women in the marketplace who are known for their unswerving integrity. Genuine, caring, honest, and trustworthy people. Businesses would clamor for that kind of leadership. Other workers would see the likeness of Christ face-to-face each day, meaning that many of them would come to know the Lord in a personal relationship.

I hope and pray that the day to equip and unleash this vast army is upon us.

Think about It

❑ Think of the most honest person you have ever met, full of integrity and character. How would you describe this person to others? How do others react when they are in his or her presence? How interested are others in listening to what this person has to say?

❑ How do you think others see you in terms of integrity? Can you identify any breach of integrity (even a small one) that you need to repair?

Notes

1. Doug Sherman and William Hendricks, *Keeping Your Ethical Edge Sharp* (Colorado Springs: NavPress, 1990), 83.

2. Max DePree, *Leadership Jazz* (New York: Dell Publishing, 1992), 220.

3. Lawrence M. Miller, *American Spirit: Visions of a New Corporate Culture* (New York: William Morrow and Company, Inc., 1984), 122.

4. Tom Peters, *Thriving on Chaos* (New York: Alfred A.Knopf, 1988), 519.

5. Paul Hawken, *Growing a Business* (New York: Simon and Schuster, 1987), 176.

6. Sherman and Hendricks, *Keeping Your Ethical Edge Sharp*, 166.

7. Peters, *Thriving on Chaos*, 522.

8. Kenneth Blanchard and Norman Vincent Peale, *The Power of Ethical Management* (New York: William Morrow and Company, Inc., 1988), 95.

9. Sherman and Hendricks, *Keeping Your Ethical Edge Sharp*, 67-8.

10. Peters, *Thriving on Chaos*, 521.

11. Miller, *American Spirit*, 132.

9

Plan for the Long Haul

....

So far in this section of the book, we've examined three godly principles that make good business sense: serving customers, loving coworkers, and developing integrity. These areas provide rich opportunities to build up our business ministry—plus they form a base for long-term company success.

The key word here is *long-term*. Although each principle can be implemented right away, at least in part, the effects of these actions on people and company performance can only be fully seen over the course of many months and years. For example, if you and I were to open a pizza shop together, our outstanding effort to win over pizza customers for life would not be seen until, over time, the same people bought pizzas from us again and again. Our well-trained and enthusiastic employees would also bear fruit gradually, with low turnover rates, happy customers, and a great opportunity to influence young people for Christ.

Unfortunately, most businesses still place the greatest importance on matters of an extremely short-term nature, such as monthly sales figures or annual profits. Management incentives and bonuses are usually based on these figures, meaning some executives go through a great deal of budget gymnastics to meet their goals at the end of a reporting period.

Is there anything wrong with this fixation on short-term profits? Isn't the whole purpose of business to make money? I'd like to answer no to those questions using the words of several respected business leaders. The only lecture statement I committed to memory during M.B.A. school came from marketing professor Hans Thoreli: "Businesses do not exist to make money. Businesses make money to remain in existence."

The wisdom of this comment has been reflected in stories of today's successful entrepreneurs. Absent from nearly every person's story is a burning desire and focus on making money. Instead, the passion centered on their products, services, or employees. Profits were seen as merely a means to keep the business going and fuel its growth.

Kenneth Blanchard and Norman Vincent Peale, both men who have made their share of profits, find the 100 percent bottom line approach to business absurd. "Managing *only* for profit is like playing tennis with your eye on the scoreboard and not on the ball." [1]

The "ball" in most businesses is the needs of its customers. When a manager only looks at the current bottom line, he or she may make little changes that help lighten this quarter's expenses but may undermine the company's ability to meet long-term customer needs. Cutting down on the number of employees staffing the customer service hot line will reduce costs, but if enough customers can't get their calls through when they have a problem, the business will be in trouble in a matter of months or years.

Long Haul Strategies

How do we develop an ability to focus on what is truly important in business for the long haul? Here are a few tips I hope you find useful:

1. *Cultivate a divine sense of patience and perseverance.* When I studied business in school, nearly every marketing text I read went over the four *P's* of marketing: product, price, place, and promotion. As foundational as those aspects are to marketing, they are trivial compared to the two *P's* of Christian living: patience and perseverance. Even in today's marketplace of unprecedented change, these long-haul characteristics are still considered virtues.

Patience is an attribute of God I value deeply, particularly during periods in my life when I've found little time for Him and stumbled into sin. His fatherly patience is present throughout the Old

Testament, as His chosen people repeatedly turned their backs on the one who had always been so faithful to them. Unfortunately, when I pray to God, I demonstrate barely a shred of His patience while waiting for Him to respond.

How important is patience? Well, Paul's famous "love is" passage in 1 Corinthians 13:4-7 begins with "love is patient." I wonder how many arguments, conflicts, and poor decisions could be avoided each day if we all had patience? According to Blanchard and Peale, most ethical deterioration in organizations can be traced to "impatience in attaining goals and objectives."[2]

If you grabbed your Bible to look up 1 Corinthians 13 or have it memorized, you'll notice Paul ends the paragraph with the other *P*, stating that love "always perseveres." In fact, the two terms are much like matching bookends or two sides of the same coin. Both traits deal with being steadfast, often in the face of tough conditions or opposition. I see perseverance as continuing to try or persist in spite of adversity, while patience has to do with trusting God to use our faithful efforts for good.

Perseverance is frequently referred to positively in the New Testament, even though it is often developed as a result of suffering or trials. Although perseverance is good in itself, it leads to even better things for Christians. In Romans 5:1-5, Paul instructs us that suffering produces perseverance, which leads to character and, ultimately, to hope. In James 1:4 we read: "Perseverance must finish its work so that you may be mature and complete, not lacking anything."

In my service to God, He has had to teach me much about patience and perseverance, particularly since I breezed through much of my youth, taking the path of least resistance. Back in 1988, God provided me with the vision and the desire to help Christians view their work as a significant ministry. I quickly set about my research. My initial timetable showed a rapid transition to a teaching and writing ministry that even included a small business—activities I planned to make my full-time occupation within a year or two.

God skillfully managed to encourage me in this ministry even as He dramatically altered my timetable. It took four years for me to teach my first class and have my first articles on work published, plus another three years before I started up my business. God's plan included more time for me to learn, prepare, and to better apply biblical principles in my own work in health care. The most important

129

lessons I have learned through this period are to be available for God's use, keep plugging away where He wants me to, and leave the results in God's capable hands.

2. *Avoid the shortsighted sins of profit squeezing and obsession with rapid growth.* Cutting back expenses to pad current profits has become so popular that companies have come up with sophisticated sounding terms to describe the practice: downsizing, rightsizing, and re-engineering the corporation. Lawrence Miller finds those practices shortsighted no matter what you call them:

> Any fool can meet a profit objective by cutting today's costs. Unfortunately, the sacrifice that is made in the cost cutting often undermines those functions (research and development or training) that have most to do with the ability of the firm to perform in the long term....While there are times when it is proper to make short-term decisions, a pattern of this behavior is quickly perceived by employees, and it properly causes them to understand that the priority of management is not the achievement of any higher goal or purpose for the firm, but the realization of short-term numbers. The same behavior should then be expected of subordinates. [3]

Sometimes cutbacks are needed during tough times to ensure company survival, but even then caution is necessary. During the first two years of HealthEast's existence, it lost over $35 million and, at one point, had only enough cash for a few days of company operations. In the early days of the firm's dramatic financial turnaround, management made the difficult decision to sell off the bulk of its diversified services division, which included growing home care, durable medical equipment, and medical transportation businesses. Although these services were considered a key to the organization's future, they would also be the easiest to sell for badly needed cash.

Fortunately for HealthEast, the proposed sale of the businesses to one buyer fell through. By this time, the corporation had reversed its financial direction and decided to hold onto these growing services. Although selling would have been preferable to going under, the company has benefited greatly from keeping all its key services.

Besides profits, the other short-term intoxicant for businesses is rapid growth. One of America's favorite types of hero is the person who begins a tiny venture out of nothing and watches it spring up overnight to become a huge enterprise. Many of us have followed closely and drawn inspiration from at least one garage to greatness business, whether it be Hewlett-Packard, Apple Computer, Inc., Microsoft, or Wal-Mart.

Entrepreneurial success has spawned an obsession with growth. Since 1982, *Inc.: The Magazine for Growing Companies* has glorified the practice with their annual Inc. 500 list of fastest growing companies. The only factor determining a company's ranking is percentage of revenue growth during the previous five years. What does it take to get on the list? Most of the time a firm won't even make the list with a strong quadrupling of sales. Imagine the blinding multiplication occurring at firms at the top of the scale, where five-year growth is well over 10,000 percent.

How fast is too fast, anyway? Certainly growth has its advantages, such as creating new jobs and, hopefully, growing profits. But is growth absolutely necessary? Although this question has often been answered affirmatively, the essential need for business growth has been challenged in recent years. According to economist Milton Friedman, "We don't have a desperate need to grow. We have a desperate desire to grow." [4]

Rapid growth can provide a thrill much like taking the most daring ride at the amusement park, only it is much more dangerous. Paul Hawken calls the time of speedy growth the "most perilous period in a company's development," because it can lead to mistakes that are masked by the firm's outward prosperity. [5] So often, today's marketplace "stars" end up being shooting stars, blazing across the headlines, then falling quickly to earth.

> **Rapid growth can provide a thrill much like taking the most daring ride at the amusement park, only it is much more dangerous.**

God's Word has never found speed desirable in matters dealing with money. According to Proverbs 21:5, "The plans of the diligent lead to profit as surely as haste leads to poverty." The best way to grow things financially, says Proverbs 13:11, is to accumulate "little by little."

Look at God's creation. Trees are among the largest and most

Plan for the Long Haul

beautiful of living things, yet many varieties take 50 to 100 years or longer to reach their full height. By contrast, the fastest grower in the human body is cancer.

Even *Inc.* has had second thoughts on growth as a goal, although for different reasons:

> Growth served as America's entrepreneurial religion during the '80s because of a particular set of conditions. Those conditions—demographic, political, and economic—no longer hold....In the coming years all-out, high-speed growth will rarely be possible. It will rarely be desirable. Small will once again be beautiful—by necessity. [6]

3. Build your business and your career upon a firm, timeless foundation, not today's latest management fad. Despite having an M.B.A. and reading much from today's business thinkers, I'm absolutely convinced that good business practices are absurdly simple to understand. Treat your customers like kings, strive to produce the best quality products/services around, and handle employees as you would your most precious resource—because they are!

While these ideas are easy to grasp, implementing them requires constant, long-term, total attention from management. Of course, many "get-it-done-yesterday" managers are apt to search for a short-cut. Because of that, a huge industry of consultants, books, and seminars has sprung up with techniques to get your business humming before the end of the fiscal year. Of course getting "optimal" results will cost you some money, since you'll want to have all the company managers trained to implement this sophisticated new program.

Over the years, the names of the latest "in" program or management fad have changed greatly. In my lifetime so far I remember seeing management by objective, zero-based budgeting, matrix management, portfolio management, one-minute managing, participative management, management by walking about, corporate re-engineering, intrapreneurship, the learning organization, and total quality management.

Most of these techniques have something useful to teach us, but none of them will work unless they are consistent with what is important to the organization and how it functions outside of this program. For instance, a managing total quality program (one of the better techniques in business today) will have a steep, uphill struggle to influence a corporation obsessed with minimizing current costs because quality improvement efforts usually require some up-front investment of time and money—plus it takes time to achieve the results.

Employees will generally follow whatever they see management pursuing over the long haul. If top management values customers or quality or employee satisfaction most (both by what they say and how they spend their time), organizational commitment to those concepts will likely be high.

> **Treat your customers like kings, strive to produce the best quality products/services around, and handle employees as you would your most precious resource— because they are!**

Maytag has spent years building a reputation for quality and dependability. Sometimes it almost appears as if they go overboard. Most companies make one grade of product for consumer use and another for commercial users. Not Maytag. The only difference between the model families put in their homes and those used by high-volume laundromats is the coin slot. For the firm's twenty-fifth anniversary of making washers, Maytag held a contest to find the oldest operating machine. Of the more than 30,000 entries received, the winner was the thirteenth one they manufactured.

4. As stewards of God's earth, our workplace practices should seek to minimize pollution, waste, and destruction of resources. Another long-haul strategy is to take care of the earth so it can sustain businesses for the next generation. Now mentioning the word *environmentalism* is enough to make many business-people cringe because many in the movement are at least as much antibusiness as they are pro-environment. We need a sense of balance when talking about the environment. Extreme environmentalists need to understand that God placed man on this earth to rule and subdue it, ruling over "every living creature" (Gen. 1:28-30; Ps. 8:6-8). All other forms of life do not have equal rights with people, although we do have responsibilities in our rule. On the other hand, some people in business need to understand that God gave us the earth to use, not use up. I think we'd be held in neglect of our stewardship role if we turned back to God a toxic earth piled high with garbage and stripped of every last trace of its resources and beauty.

Some environmentalists predict that we are in our last generation of business as usual; that, despite our efforts to recycle and be "green," the earth will soon lose its ability to sustain our current resource-draining economy.

Are such alarming statements true? I don't know, although I suspect the truth lies somewhere between those who say the earth has just about had it and those who believe technology will fix any problems we have. I also suspect there are limits to how many landfills we can create, how many forests we can clear-cut, and how many species we can let pass into extinction.

Since none of us knows when Christ will return to earth, it would be wise to treat the planet as if it will need to last a while longer. We should all avoid excessive pollution of the air and water. Make products that last, can be reused/recycled, or can decompose easily.

In recent years, the computer industry has made great strides in reducing waste. During the early days of personal computers, the waste was quite disturbing. Early models were generally well-made, but had little capacity to expand as technology improved. This book was written on a Leading Edge XT-compatible, a nice computer back when I bought it, but a dinosaur in today's market. Since this computer cannot be upgraded to run the latest version of my favorite word processing software, I plan to replace it after I finish writing these pages. Fortunately, today's computers contain far greater capacity for expansion, meaning they won't end up on the trash heap for many years to come. My hope is for all industries to reduce waste that quickly.

> **I think we'd be held in neglect of our stewardship role if we turned back to God a toxic earth piled high with garbage and stripped of every last trace of its resources and beauty.**

Besides reducing the negative impact on the environment, it would be great if entrepreneurs would emerge to help improve things. Bob Laing is trying to do just that. As founder and president of Clean-Flo Laboratories, Inc., Bob has applied his engineering talents, together with God's leading, to come up with a means of speeding up the natural inversion process for cleaning up a body of water. Using special infusion pumps and microorganism supplements, Clean-Flo can turn a lifeless, mucky lake into one that is crystal clear and teeming with fish and other aquatic life. Although Bob would disdain being identified as an environmentalist—a movement he feels has strayed from what is important—his company has cleaned up thousands of polluted lakes, rivers, and ponds throughout the world.

5. Make your plans flexible so God can lead you. Despite the desirability in business to be fully "at the helm," it is important that we submit to God's will. Proverbs 16:9 says, "In his heart a man plans his course, but the LORD determines his steps." God has mapped out His grand "strategic plan" for this world, and we're all to play a part in its implementation. Rarely, however, does God map out His will for us in neat, five-year increments. Instead, He desires us to walk with Him in faith, trusting that our Father will let us know the next step to take.

Despite this knowledge, it's so easy to catch ourselves plotting out our future as if we are in control of everything. We make our plans and decisions, then ask God to bless them. We forget that our plans for tomorrow or next year may need to change substantially, depending on what God intends to do. I imagine that Noah had some worthy goals and plans for his life on the day God spoke to him; probably none of them dealt with building an ark for a flood. Talk about a change of plans! Just as in Noah's case, to ignore what God is doing in the world around us would be extremely foolish.

God can inform us of our need to alter our plans through many means, individuals, and circumstances. We need to be open to God's leading rather than stubbornly clinging to our own ideas. Bob Laing did not have lake cleaning in mind when he first developed his "clean-flo" technology; God brought him a customer who asked if he could clean up a murky lake.

My own plans and timetables have become more flexible because God has changed them so often. In fact, I was very close to implementing my business plan when I received the go-ahead to write this book. I had to dramatically alter my plans for 1994 to complete the task God had set before me.

Being Long-Haul in a Short-Term Company

How can we implement these biblical long-haul concepts if we work for a company whose only concern is this month's sales and profits? It can be done, but it won't always be easy. Start with prayer for wisdom for your company leaders—and for yourself to influence them. Then, if possible, seek to find a project to demonstrate the value of a longer-term focus. Perhaps it is something as elaborate as a high-quality new product designed with customer value in mind, instead of low cost. Or maybe it can be something simple like a training program you begin in your spare time. It will take time, but creating a small, long-haul success story may convince the company to let you or others attempt to duplicate the feat.

Another strategy is to try to position yourself in the organization where you can influence others in this alternative approach. Anyone who hires, supervises, trains, or communicates to large numbers of employees (or to employees in influential positions) can make a substantial impact, even in very short-term organizations. I've never hired or supervised many employees, but I've been involved in their training, facilitated many planning meetings, and had some influence over internal and external communications. Occasionally, I feel like a rejected prophet, but often I can see some impact from my efforts.

Other times, however, an employer can be so obsessed with squeezing out short-term profits that it's killing the organization—and you may need to leave the sinking ship. My friend the auto salesperson could not change the customer-manipulation strategy of his employer so, over time, he realized he needed a change of scenery.

The long-haul approach is not just a good idea for the marketplace. It should be present in all aspects of a Christian's life. For our God has eternity as His primary frame of reference, not next week or even next year. We all need to cultivate a more divine sense of patience, understanding that much of what is worthwhile in life takes time to develop.

Think about It

❏ How patient are you in achieving your goals in life?

❏ Do your plans include enough flexibility to allow God to influence and change them according to His will?

Notes

1. Kenneth Blanchard and Norman Vincent Peale, *The Power of Ethical Management* (New York: William Morrow and Company, Inc., 1988), 106.

2. Ibid., 110.

3. Lawrence M. Miller, *American Spirit: Visions of a New Corporate Culture* (New York: William Morrow and Company, Inc., 1984), 127.

4. Milton Friedman, *The Macmillan Book of Business and Economic Quotations*, Michael Jackman, ed. (New York: Macmillan Publishing Company, 1984), 104.

5. Paul Hawken, *Growing a Business* (New York: Simon and Schuster, 1987), 92.

6. John Case and Elizabeth Conlin, "Second Thoughts on Growth," *Inc.* (March 1991): 50.

Part 3

Challenging Issues for Executives

In the final section of this book, we'll examine some issues that are key to successfully living out our faith in the marketplace.

❑ How can we be sure to seek and follow God's will, especially with major decisions?

❑ We know what success means in the world's eyes, but what is success from God's point of view?

❑ What should we do when the workload keeps piling higher and higher—and we feel ourselves wearing down under the strain?

❑ Is there any gain in striving for the top of the corporate ladder or, as an entrepreneur, building your own ladder?

❑ Can Christians be active and effective witnesses at the office without using uncomfortable, hard-sell techniques?

❑ What activities can I start doing tomorrow to begin building up my ministry at work?

Most of these issues will likely assume significance at some point in anyone's career. Each topic could merit a book of its own, so these chapters represent a quick overview.

10

Handling Tough
Business Decisions

••

The previous section of this book examined how to perform our everyday work tasks as part of our service to God. Being a servant to customers, loving coworkers, developing integrity, and focusing on the long haul are sound biblical strategies for our business ministry.

Inevitably, however, you will face larger issues or decisions during your career. Perhaps it will be a new but dramatically different job opportunity—one offering additional risks as well as rewards. Maybe you'll have to decide whether to fire an employee who is likable, obedient, and hardworking, but not competent enough to do the job well. Or someday you may be asked to "shade the truth" or "fudge the numbers," perhaps in such a subtle manner that no one else in the firm sees it as dishonest—it is just the way the game is played. Of course, your refusal to play could be interpreted as insubordination.

How do we as Christians handle the bigger issues? Many decisions we face do not appear black and white at first glance, not lending themselves to one-minute management techniques. A clear "do" or "do not" may not come to mind from Scripture, making quick insight into God's will difficult.

So what goes into making a sound decision? Here are five important steps:

1. **Research the situation.** Knowing the relevant facts is always important to making decisions. Research sounds like such an obvi-

ous step, but it's easy to be lazy. As Christians, we sometimes fall into the trap of substituting prayer for research. Just ask God what to do, and He'll show us the way. Yet, without the facts, we may not even know what to pray about. Also, God's will and answer for our decision may well be found in the facts themselves.

> **As Christians, we sometimes fall into the trap of substituting prayer for research.**

The Bible—especially Proverbs—is quite clear about the importance of knowledge in our quest for discernment:

> Every prudent man acts out of knowledge, but a fool exposes his folly (Prov. 13:16).

> The discerning heart seeks knowledge, but the mouth of a fool feeds on folly (Prov. 15:14).

> The heart of the discerning acquires knowledge; the ears of the wise seek it out (Prov. 18:15).

Changing jobs is one decision where acquiring knowledge can greatly aid the decision-making process. Would any of us take a new position based solely on what was printed in a newspaper classified advertisement? Of course not. We'd try to learn as much about the position and the company as possible. In fact, the further along most people are with their careers, the more information they seek about new opportunities. A friend of mine in retail management has changed companies several times. Because of previous experiences with retailers who treat their store managers poorly, my friend researches each prospective employer more carefully as his career progresses, including calls to randomly selected managers to learn what's not in the corporate brochure.

In most business and personal decisions, the more information you have, the easier it is to discern the best decision. Sometimes just one obscure fact can make the correct path obvious. For example, in the deadly space shuttle accident years ago, one piece of information on a problem component placed in the hands of those who made the launch decision would have saved the lives of the crew.

2. Search for applicable Bible wisdom. The Bible is not meant to be an abstract collection of stories and parables. God's Word is intended to be put "into practice" (Matt. 7:24), serving as a "light" or guide for our path of life (Ps. 119:105) and equipping us for every good work (2 Tim. 3:16-17). I cannot recall a situation or decision in my life where I could not find some helpful principle in the pages of the Bible.

If you have not already done so, I recommend an investment in a good Bible resource library, which might include a concordance, Bible dictionary, Bible encyclopedia, a comprehensive commentary, and a good topical or study Bible. Don't worry about buying another bookcase to house all this knowledge; today you can purchase it all on a single CD-ROM disk for your computer.

Once you've dug through God's Word to gain insight for a particular situation, the wisdom gained often stays with you for a lifetime. One verse that has long guided me in financial matters has been Proverbs 22:7: "The rich rule over the poor, and the borrower is servant to the lender."

Keeping that verse in mind has made me very hesitant about going into debt in either my personal or business dealings. I've seen too many families and businesses collapse under a mountain of debt. If I had burdened myself with a heavier debt load over the years, my career would probably have taken a different path, more financially driven and less enjoyable.

3. Pray for wisdom and ask for the prayers of others. Proverbs 2 extols the benefits of God's wisdom, which allows us to "understand what is right and just and fair—every good path" (v. 9). It also serves to protect and guard us from the ways of the wicked and the path of adultery. All this great wisdom is available to those who ask God in faith, according to James 1:5-8.

When we pray to God about a decision or situation, it is important that we be open to His leading, instead of merely asking Him to bless and go along with what we have already decided. Too often in my prayer life, I catch myself sounding as if I'm ordering off the menu at a restaurant: "I'd like my day to go well, help me get through this presentation, help me get caught up in my paperwork, give me safety on this upcoming business trip."

The wise man or woman will pray for God's will to be done,

seeking to choose the course that will most honor Him. Ron Klug notes that, since even Christ submitted to the will of the Father, we need to be the ones willing to change. "While we can and should bring all our needs and desires to God, our prayer is not an attempt to bend God to our will, but to bend our will to his." [1]

Besides our own prayers, asking others to pray for us is also wise. I used to be more hesitant in sharing personal prayer requests with others, thinking it to be more self-centered than praying for someone's salvation. Over time, my experience in small groups taught me that praying for each other's needs benefits all those involved because seeing how God answers prayer strengthens our faith.

4. Seek out wise counsel. It is amazing how a crisis, particularly one charged with emotion, can turn the most logical mind to mush. We go over and over the issue in our heads until all clear perspective is lost; therefore, it is invaluable to talk over issues with others, especially mature Christian brothers and sisters. They can offer needed empathy, share how they faced similar circumstances, give advice, and even rebuke us if we're drifting off course.

The Book of Proverbs is again a wealth of wisdom on seeking counsel:

Plans fail for lack of counsel, but with many advisers they succeed (Prov. 15:22).

Listen to advice and accept instruction, and in the end you will be wise (Prov. 19:20).

The way of a fool seems right to him, but a wise man listens to advice (Prov. 12:15).

Stay away from a foolish man, for you will not find knowledge on his lips (Prov. 14:7).

That last passage suggests we should be very careful about whom we choose as our advisers. Bad advice, if followed, can take us further off the right path; on the other hand, wise Christian counsel is a valuable asset.

Jerry Dettinger of ParaBody Fitness became such a firm believer in seeking good counsel that he has formalized the process, creating a five-person council of advisers who help to hold him accountable in running the business. He put together the group with a great deal of prayer, choosing individuals with a solid business background in addition to a mature Christian faith.

5. Find time to think and reflect. Although occasional situations call for immediate action, most decisions allow time for thought and reflection. Don't be tempted by a business culture that often equates leadership with firm, snap decision-making skills. Whenever possible, take time to let your thoughts simmer over a tough business issue for awhile. Proverbs 14:8 notes: "The wisdom of the prudent is to give thought to their ways" while Proverbs 19:2 warns that it is not good "to be hasty and miss the way."

> **Don't be tempted by a business culture that often equates leadership with firm, snap decision-making skills.**

For example, I've learned, for the most part, not to set a deadline on large work projects until I have time to think about the tasks they entail and what else is on my calendar. Without taking time to think, I frequently commit to a completion date that can be reached only with great personal stress.

Some issues require more time for reflection than others. Decisions dealing with career direction or major business strategy may require extended time out of the office to think. Companies schedule retreats outside the office to ponder and plan for the future—so should individuals.

Also, taking time to reflect gets us to sit still long enough for God to speak to us. Too often I catch myself praying for wisdom and guidance; then I go off and make a decision without a pause. God does not always provide answers with the speed of a McDonald's drive-through window. If we truly want Christ to be Lord of our whole life, we need to allow time for Him to direct us.

The career decision that led to this book, among other things, came about after lengthy periods of reflection. Back in 1986, during a long winter hike in the woods, I committed my fledgling writing efforts to whatever God would lead me to write, instead of the pursuit of a national best-seller. During the next year, God helped me to understand that my arena for ministry was to be in the business world, not the pulpit. Finally, in 1988, in the midst of a vacation that followed a three-day silent retreat, I finally understood my writing and teaching calling: to help businesspeople and other Christian workers see their everyday work as ministry. It took a lengthy incubation period to get to the decision, but that time allowed me to better see where God was guiding me.

Don't Rely on Just One Step

Sometimes it is tempting to take a shortcut in the decision-making process. Perhaps we'll only go to a close friend for advice. Or just mull the problem over for an evening. Maybe we only look until we find some shred of evidence that supports the decision we intended to make all along, then quickly end our research lest we discover something contradictory. Or we just wait for a "good sign," an event or set of circumstances that makes our decision easier.

According to Henry Blackaby and Claude King, in their book, *Experiencing God*, these one-dimensional approaches stem more likely from a self-centered motivation rather than a sincere desire to seek God's will:

> You must be careful to identify God's initiative and distinguish it from your selfish desires. A self-centered life will have a tendency to confuse its selfish desire with God's will. Circumstances, for instance, cannot always be a clear direction for God's leadership. "Open" and "closed doors" are not always indications of God's directions. In seeking God's direction, check to see that prayer, the Scripture, and circumstances agree in the direction you sense God leading you. [2]

In seeking God's will as we grapple with work issues, it is important to look for agreement among the five steps discussed earlier, instead of relying on just one. In fact, if Jim Bever had relied on only one of those steps during a crisis in his landscaping business in the early 1980s, he feels he would have missed God's leading.

Jim's business got caught in the transition between a period of high inflation and the deep recession that followed. With prices rising so fast, the common fiscal wisdom was to be highly leveraged, buying whatever the business needed on credit before the price went up again. Before the economy hit the wall, his expanding company was projected to hit $1 million in sales, aided in part by a $60,000 line of credit he had just obtained from the bank.

When the recession hit, many families put off landscaping projects for better economic times. As revenues came in at only about 60 percent of projections, Jim knew he was in big trouble. Despite chopping expenses wherever he could, he couldn't even keep up with the interest payments on his line of credit—no small task given that interest rates were hovering around 20 percent.

With the end in sight, Jim had a decision to make. He spent the next six to eight months "getting as much input and information as I could." He researched all financial and legal options. He met with attorneys, as well as many Christian brothers and pastors. Most told him to pull the plug, declare bankruptcy, and start over.

Rather than following this advice, Jim continued to get input. He read the Word, studied the writings of Larry Burkett and other Christian financial writers, and prayed. The more input he received, "the more I really believed that God wanted me not to go bankrupt, just to be honorable and honor the debt I had."

The wisdom of this decision may not have been apparent right away. "They ended up taking everything I had except the furniture," said Bever. His land, house, inventory, and equipment were sold to reduce his $310,000 mountain of debt to just under $100,000. After that he worked three days a week for a friend in the banking supplies business, while landscaping the rest of the time to continue paying off his debts.

It took many years of sacrifice to honor those debts, but he feels confident God wanted him to take that route—and it has born fruit. Nearly all his vendors have stuck by him, having learned that Jim Bever will honor his debts.

Use God's Tools for Making Decisions

Are you facing a major decision or issue in your life? Whenever the situation arises, we need to remember to use what God provides for us to live according to His will: the Bible, prayer, our minds, and the sage advice of others. As we use God's tools to make wise decisions, those around us will feel His impact, and our ministry in business will be strengthened.

Think about It

❑   Think back to the last major business decision you made. How many of the five steps in the chapter did you use as you determined your course of action? What other input did you use? Are you satisfied with the choice you made? Do you think God is?

Notes

1. Ron Klug, *Bible Readings on Prayer* (Minneapolis: Augsburg Publishing House, 1986), 15.

2. Henry T. Blackaby and Claude V. King, *Experiencing God* (Nashville: Broadman & Holman Publishers, 1994), 70.

Chapter 11

A Godly Approach to Success

··

In today's marketplace, Christ's Sermon on the Mount—in which He blessed the poor, hungry, and meek—might face a chilly reception. The higher echelons of corporate America still largely see such talk as consolation for losers, for those people who lack the ambition to carve out their own mark of success in this world. Now if a speaker wanted to get a warmer response, he or she might want to recite a little of what I call the "Boardroom Beatitudes":

Blessed are the rich, who can make all their fantasies a reality.

Blessed are the famous, who can gloat while the world strains to know their secrets.

Blessed are the bold, whose self-confidence will take them far.

Blessed are the powerful, who have control over people and events.

The contrast between Christ's beatitudes and the world's view is striking. As Christians, we find ourselves attempting to juggle what the Bible tells us to seek with what we've learned are the keys to success in our culture. According to Tony Campolo in his book, *The Success Fantasy*, the two sets of success criteria are too different to be blended:

149

Because the world sees wealth, power, and prestige as the indicators of success, we have been conditioned to seek them with all of our might. But our Lord has a different criteria for evaluating success. He calls us away from society's symbols of success and urges us to seek after "His kingdom and His righ-teous-ness" (Matt. 6:33). Many who are considered least important by society may find themselves sit-

> **Seeking power and prestige is good, we tell ourselves, because prominent individuals will have a broader wit-ness.**

ting in places of honor at the great banquet feast in the world to come. [1]

Unfortunately, as Christians, we have been more influenced by the world's view of success than we have been effective in changing it. Seeking power and prestige is good, we tell ourselves, because prominent individuals will have a broader witness. Piling up wealth is okay too, just as long as we don't love it too much. Besides, those added riches can be given to further the Gospel—after the mansion and our top-of-the-line Mercedes is paid off.

Taken to its extreme, Christians will end up seeking the same things and living the same way as everyone else, except we claim to be "saved." Will non-Christians believe us when we tell them Jesus changes lives if the only visible change they see is that we frequent churches instead of bars?

Society's success indicators have always been a temptation for me, as well as for most other Christians I know in business. Let's look more closely at each element—power, prestige, and money—in the critical light of God's Word.

Power

Power is something everyone seems to want, particularly if it is an election year. The desire to be in control, in charge, the top dog is appealing to many. After all, those who are in power set the agenda and usually make the rules. I remember a line Mel Brooks said in one of his movies, "It's good to be the king."

Even Christians see the benefit of being in authority, seeking top business and political positions to make positive changes. Also, the visibility of those in power brings about potential opportunities for being a witness, good or bad.

Although the concept is appealing, the corridors of power can be a brutal place. Competition can be cutthroat because those in authority will not yield without a fight and those who want to ascend don't care what it takes to get there.

If you ever want to get a taste for raw power at work, get involved in a major political campaign—something I've tried on several occasions. In the early stages of a campaign, workers jockey for important positions, since the ultimate carrot is to gain a staff position, should the candidate win. After the team is established, strong turf boundaries are set and new talent is rarely sought—just people to make phone calls and stuff envelopes. And should the candidate fall well behind in the polls, watch the power-seekers desert in droves.

Do I sound a little cynical? I lost my idealism at an early age after years of being surrounded by those clawing their way to the top. I still remember my frustration in serving on a campaign for U.S. Senate, where I held a minor position on the campaign "team." Even though it didn't fall within my assigned duties, I repeatedly offered to pitch in with the important task of writing positioning statements on issues. Despite possessing what I thought were reasonable credentials (awards in editorial and opinion writing, and an author of a piece of the state party's platform), I was politely but firmly excluded from contributing in that manner. I'm afraid I don't volunteer much politically anymore.

What does the Bible say about power? In Romans 13:1, we are told to submit to those in authority, because the authorities "have been established by God." Unless those in power attempt to force us into sin, we must submit to them out of respect, whether they seem worthy of that respect or not.

If we should happen to be in a position of authority, we are taught not to use it for our own gain but to serve others. In Mark 10:42-45, Jesus says we should not "lord" our power over people, but must be a servant and "slave of all."

Therefore, power is not something to be sought after as a badge of career success. Instead, we should humbly accept it from a desire to serve others. I think Peter's instruction to elders summarizes a godly approach for those in power:

> Be shepherds of God's flock that is under your care, serving as overseers—not because you must, but because you are willing, as God wants you to be; not greedy for money, but eager to serve; not lording it over those entrusted to you, but being examples to the flock (1 Peter 5:2-3).

Prestige

The dictionary defines *prestige* as influence rising from reputation or esteem. Beyond that, prestige is a difficult trait to nail down in our fad-conscious culture. What is trendy changes almost monthly it seems, and so does who is in the limelight, who is being listened to. Usually, however, those with significant influence these days include athletes, entertainers, and others with significant amounts of power and/or money.

Even in Christian circles, prestige can be a factor. Often sports figures, entertainers, and business leaders are a big draw at evangelism events because their success in one arena makes others willing to listen to what they have to say in another arena.

When I was in M.B.A. school, prestige went to those who were able to obtain job offers from blue chip companies or those firms involved in "hot" industries. For marketing students at that time, the ultimate achievement was to get an offer from Procter & Gamble. Sure, new hires there were known to work like dogs, madly scrambling to be one of the elite who would move up to the next rung in the organization. No one needed to worry, though, because P & G experience would open the door for almost any product management position in the country.

Is having others view us highly wrong? Of course not. What is wrong, however, is how badly we desire that prestige and what we might compromise to get it. After all, gaining status is mainly about feeding our own selfish ego. This vanity caught Paul's attention when he wrote in Philippians 2:3-4, "Do nothing out of selfish ambition or vain conceit, but in humility consider others better than yourselves. Each of you should look not only to your own interests, but also to the interests of others."

Besides humility, the Bible teaches a rejection of the world's praises, because "what is highly valued among men is detestable in God's sight" (Luke 16:15). In fact, Jesus told His disciples that if they had belonged to the world it would love them but, because of Him, "the world hates you" (John 15:19). Some leaders in Jesus' day would not confess their faith publicly out of fear, "for they loved praise from men more than praise from God" (John 12:42-43). As our country has become increasingly hostile toward Christianity, we find ourselves frequently forced to choose whose love we seek most.

> **As our country has become increasingly hostile toward Christianity, we find ourselves frequently forced to choose whose love we seek most.**

Prestige and a positive self-image are important to many people. Yet, as one made in God's image, gaining status from others and self-contained personal improvement programs seems silly. As Christians, the only image we should seek to reflect is that of God, and the primary influence we should desire to exert is that of a directional beacon to Jesus Christ for others to see and follow.

Money

An ungodly attitude toward money is perhaps the most significant area of temptation and sin in our culture. It is a universal problem, affecting both rich and poor, Christian and non-Christian.

If you read much of today's trendwatchers, you might conclude that our preoccupation with wealth is behind us. The 1980s was labeled the decade of greed, meaning the 1990s would be a time for folks to simplify their lives and concentrate on what's important. Indeed, instead of spending their

> **An ungodly attitude toward money is perhaps the most significant area of temptation and sin in our culture.**

time and money out on the town, people started to stay home more. However, that fueled a remodeling boom as homeowners created spacious bedroom suites, media rooms filled with state-of-the-art electronic gadgetry, and kitchens that would make Julia Child misty-eyed.

Another trend, the renewed popularity of bicycling, was supposed to signal a return to healthier, simpler days gone by. Of course, those old-fashioned bikes didn't have $2,000 price tags and require outfits and accessories that cost even more.

No, greed is not gone; it will always be with us. Unfortunately, it seems that little is being done to counter it, even within the church. Worse yet, the views of those expounding the "prosperity gospel" have crept into some Christian circles. Their "teaching" is based on the belief that God wants us all to be rich and, if you ask and have faith, He will provide everything you ask for and then some.

The prosperity gospel is one of those "you can have it all" formulas that has always been popular. It intuitively has some appeal, particularly during months when the checkbook balance disappears under an avalanche of bills. However, the prosperity teaching is filled with problems.

❑ God seems to be at our beck and call, like a genie waiting to grant our wish. This does not sound like the God who brings both good times and bad (Ecc. 7:14) and allows trials so we can become mature and complete (James 1:2-4).

❑ It incorrectly assumes that God's blessings are mainly financial. One pastor wrote an article in which he inserted the words "empowered to prosper" in parentheses each time the word "blessing" appeared in a Bible passage, with prosperity of course meaning material riches. However, Jesus taught us to store up treasures in heaven, not on earth (Matt. 6; Luke 12). We are to focus on God, not on things we need, for God will provide what He determines we need.

❑ These teachings ignore biblical warnings on wealth. Riches are dangerous because they can lead to pride. In Ezekiel 28:4-5, the prophet condemned the wealth of the port city of Tyre, saying, "Because of your wealth your heart has grown proud." The writer of Proverbs 30:8-9 asks God for neither "poverty nor riches" because too much wealth can cause people to disown their Lord.

❑ Nearly all the characters of the New Testament were relatively poor, despite God's blessing. Jesus had few if any possessions; His disciples left behind whatever modest prosperity they had to follow Him; the early believers were generally poor, and those with wealth often sold their possessions to give to the rest. Despite this, Paul praises God in Ephesians 1:3 for blessing them "with every spiritual blessing in Christ." Francis Bacon wrote, "Prosperity is the blessing of the Old Testament; adversity is the blessing of the New." Sharing in the suffering and persecution Christ faced on earth is perhaps a more likely and worthy blessing than outrageous wealth.

More Biblical Wisdom on Money

The Bible is loaded with teaching on money, so I'll limit our discussion to highlights. Having wealth is no sin, but those "eager to get rich" will be punished (Prov. 28:20). Those who love money and wealth are "never satisfied," no matter how much they amass (Ecc. 5:10; 6:7). And as we already learned, too much wealth can lead to pride (Prov. 30:8-9; Ezek. 28:4-5). Even the seemingly simple act of wanting to be rich can be dangerous, according to 1 Timothy 6:9-10:

> People who want to get rich fall into temptation and a trap and into many foolish and harmful desires that plunge men into ruin and destruction. For the love of money is a root of all kinds of evil. Some people, eager for money, have wandered from the faith and pierced themselves with many griefs.

James 5:1-6 also contains a strong warning to the rich, particularly those who hoard their wealth, accumulate money by taking advantage of their workers and live in "luxury and self-indulgence."

People will do scary things to each other in order to acquire or hold onto money. I heard about one couple who sued another couple—who had been close friends—after their friends won $7 million in the lottery. The suit claimed there was an "agreement" to split the money should any of them ever win. Not knowing the couples, it

155   *A Godly Approach to Success*

is hard to determine who was the most greedy. If all parties had orginally agreed to divide the winnings, it's sad to see the "winners" decide that half of $7 million wasn't enough, elbowing their neighbors out of what they had promised because their word was not legally binding. It would be equally pathetic to see a friendship destroyed for a piece of someone else's windfall if there were no agreement outside of a casual comment.

Money was a frequent topic in Christ's teachings, with Matthew 6 being a good example. Christians are to store up treasures in heaven, not on earth (vv. 19-20) because "where your treasure is, there your heart will be also" (v. 21). In verse 24, Jesus says we must make a choice: we cannot serve both God and money. Money can easily become an idol or a god to us, crowding Jesus out of our heart and directing us on a path of sin.

Instead, we are not to worry about material things but to keep our focus on God, seeking his kingdom first (vv. 25-34). According to John White, we are called to follow Christ's example of love and self-giving, "not caring whether we be poor or rich so long as we follow Him and do His will." [2]

Christian Success

If worldly symbols of success are not suited for Christians, what kind of a success should we seek? According to Dr. William Cook, Christian success "involves the continued achievement of being the person God wants me to be, and the continued achievement of established goals which God helps me set." [3]

Conceptually, then, Christian success is simple: be the people God created us to be and do His will. Doing that requires a total focus on God, instead of the world, meaning our relationship with Him will assume top priority in our life.

The successful Christian will find balance in his or her life and ministry, devoting adequate time for prayer, family, work, church, and other service in the community. The successful Christian will, like Paul in Philippians 4:12, learn to be content in every situation. The successful Christian knows everything belongs to God, discovering what A.W. Tozer calls "the blessedness of possessing nothing," and living with both material self-discipline and generosity. [4]

As I mentioned earlier in the chapter, Christian outreach efforts often attract audiences using high-profile individuals who look successful in worldly terms but are Christians. According to Larry Burkett, it might be wise to instead provide visibility to the uncommon person who will buck the world's success standards:

> Christian leaders in business and ministry seem bent on demonstrating how rich God can make them. But I find very few unsaved people who are impressed by a Christian's affluence. They have seen enough affluence in the world around them to be convinced that godly people aren't the only ones who accumulate money. What does impress both the unsaved and saved alike are those rare individuals who have learned to control their lifestyles and use the abundance they have to help others and spread God's Word. [5]

For me, the best opportunity I've had so far to share my faith occurred when I reduced my working hours at HealthEast. After six years of service, I created a less prestigious position for myself, one that no longer involved supervising others. Combined with the pay cut, I had given up ground on every one of today's success factors—and people wanted to know why. Since the change, I've had more opportunities to share my faith than in all the previous years of full-time employment. Sometimes being the oddball pays off.

As we go through our working lives, we need to challenge ourselves periodically by asking the question: Which success model does my life most closely match—the world's or God's?

Think about It

❑ How much do power and prestige matter to you?

❑ How much does acquiring and managing wealth figure in your life and goals?

❑ Take a moment to reflect on your goals for your life and career.

Will achieving these goals mean that your success will match the world's standards or God's standard?

Notes

1. Anthony Campolo, Jr., *The Success Fantasy* (Wheaton, Ill.: Victor Books, 1980), 17.

2. John White, *The Golden Cow: Materialism in the Twentieth-Century Church* (Downers Grove, Ill.: Inter-Varsity Press, 1979), 58.

3. William H. Cook, *Success, Motivation, and the Scriptures* (Nashville: Broadman Press, 1974), 44.

4. A.W. Tozer, *The Pursuit of God* (Harrisburg, Pa.: Christian Publications, Inc., 1948), 21.

5. Larry Burkett, *Business by the Book* (Nashville: Thomas Nelson Publishers, 1990), 44.

12

Avoiding Work Addiction

···

Judy glanced at her alarm clock and groaned. She had hit the snooze alarm not once but twice in her efforts to gain consciousness. This would definitely affect her family's split-second Sunday morning timing.

She poked Steve just hard enough to gain his attention. He had arrived home last night from an extended business trip, which was evident in his glazed-over eyes and groggy expression as he turned his head and nodded at his wife.

That was her cue to rouse the rest of the family. Judy rolled out of bed into her slippers and threw a robe over her shoulders as she rushed into the hallway. The door to Jenny's room was already open—and the main bathroom door shut—which meant her twelve-year-old was well on her way to using up all the hot water. Eric and Jeremy usually required more effort to rouse, sometimes to the point of pulling off sheets and blankets so they had no way left to shut out the world.

With her boys sitting up in bed and grumbling, Judy retraced her steps, knocked on the bathroom door to speed Jenny up, and poked her head in the bedroom to see if Steve had moved. The sound of running water in the master bathroom was an encouraging sign, so Judy could now hurry downstairs to start breakfast.

First priority was to get the coffeepot dripping, so she and Steve would be ready to tackle the day. Next came the French toast and sausages.

Steve was first to stumble down the stairs, grabbing a cup of coffee with one hand and slowly setting the table with the other. By the time the first batch of toast was done, the entire family was assembled.

As she dipped the last of the bread in the batter, Judy glanced at her watch and grimaced. Steve volunteered to finish with the cooking and cleanup while his wife rushed upstairs to get dressed.

At 8:58 A.M. Steve maneuvered their minivan into the circle in front of the church entrance. Judy rushed the rest of the family through the front door and past potential distractions to get them promptly into their chairs.

During the church service, Judy couldn't keep her mind from wandering to thoughts of all the things to be done today. There was lunch with the Andersons, billings from her home-based business, and restocking their ever-dwindling grocery supplies. Also, Steve had to go into the office for a few hours to catch up with paperwork, which made Judy primary chauffeur for the kids.

Judy tried to push those frantic thoughts aside and focus on the sermon, but the next words out of the pastor's mouth were "Let us pray."

Are Judy and Steve typical Christians? I think many of us recognize the frenzied pace of this Sunday morning, if not the activities themselves. We live in a fast-moving culture, where the treadmill seems to speed up every year.

Unfortunately, the pace is taking its toll. According to a poll by the Roper Organization, 42 percent of respondents often feel stress at the end of the day. What causes that stress? For 36 percent of the sample, the amount of money to live on was a major cause of stress which, thinking back to the last chapter, is no great surprise. The next two causes of stress are related: not having enough time (28 percent) and the amount of work to do (24 percent).[1]

The marketplace is full of stress. I can't count the number of stories I've read about new businesses where the founder talks about working 100-hour weeks in the early years, cutting back only a few hours after the venture took off. In large companies, tough competition and periodic layoffs keep the staff lean and overwhelmed. During graduate school, I traveled for a day-long interview at General Mills, in Minneapolis. My most vivid memory of the day was a comment from a transplanted Californian, who said she liked the long, cold winters because then she didn't feel upset about working through her evenings and weekends.

Christians in business often have it worse. In addition to long hours at work, we add all the demands of our Christian environment, such as church work, evangelism, and Bible study. For a while, we assume our schedule will ease up after we complete the current round of projects, but more work waits for us, and we never catch up. Some of us are willing participants in this never-ending cycle of labor, having been brought up with a strong work ethic; some are victims of circumstances. Either way, we eventually get so addicted to work that when we try to relax, we feel guilty.

Most committed Christians I know have jam-packed schedules and often appear frazzled, an expression I've noticed in the mirror a few times over the years. In fact, when I teach about work at church, nothing has generated more classroom interest than the subject of rest.

Work addiction and lack of rest have a greater impact than simply making us tired. If, for example, we are putting in too many hours on the job, our ministry will be out of balance, leading us to ignore, most likely, our family or personal time with God.

Often, we convince ourselves that being swamped with projects is okay since, after all, we're doing it in God's service. Unfortunately, according to Doug Sherman and William Hendricks, God is not the One who is pleased with our heavy load:

> If idle hands are the devil's workshop, then overly busy hands are his recreation. He loves to see people too busy to take time for God, too hurried to give any thought to the moral and ethical dimensions of what they're doing. [2]

Rest in the Bible

With sin affecting our workplaces and work habits, it is important to fully understand the cycle of work and rest God intends for us. Work is valuable in God's eyes. Overwork, however, usually stems from less than noble motives such as financial gain, career advancement, guilt, or trying to prove to ourselves that we are worthy of God's grace. In Proverbs 23:4 we are taught not to wear ourselves out to get rich, but "have the wisdom to show restraint." Psalm 127:2 calls "in vain" the efforts of those who rise early and stay up late in their toil, "for He grants sleep to those He loves."

God lays out His cycle of work and rest for people beginning with the beginning—the act of creation in Genesis. God rested on the seventh day, reflected upon all He had done and concluded that it was good. Certainly our all-powerful God wasn't tired, but He modeled the practice of rest for His people to follow, as we see in Exodus 31:15-17:

> **Often, we convince ourselves that being swamped with projects is okay since, after all, we're doing it in God's service.**

For six days, work is to be done, but the seventh day is a Sabbath of rest, holy to the LORD. Whoever does any work on the Sabbath day must be put to death. The Israelites are to observe the Sabbath, celebrating it for the generations to come as a lasting covenant. It will be a sign between Me and the Israelites forever, for in six days the LORD made the heavens and the earth, and on the seventh day He abstained from work and rested.

Those of us who feel guilty about resting should be glad we weren't Israelites because guilt was associated with never resting, and working on the Sabbath was a *capital* offense. Rest was not just an option, even during the busiest times of the year. Those with rural backgrounds know that the plowing and harvest seasons mean long hours for farmers, yet Exodus 34:21 commanded a day of rest even during these times.

> **To dismiss the cycle of work and rest that started with Creation would be a serious mistake.**

Does the Old Testament Sabbath law apply today? Since we are no longer under the Law as Christians, working on Sunday or any other particular day of the week could not be considered a sin (and certainly not a capital offense). However, to dismiss the cycle of work and rest that started with Creation would be a serious mistake. Without a regular break from our work, we lose perspective and soon begin to run out of steam. If I work too strenuously for even two weeks without a day of rest, I see my energy level dip and feel early signs of burnout.

Although stepping back from our work is an important aspect of rest, we have a special rest available from our Lord:

> Come to Me, all you who are weary and burdened, and I will give you rest. Take My yoke upon you and learn from Me, for I am gentle and humble in heart, and you will find rest for your souls. For My yoke is easy and My burden is light (Matt. 11:28-30).

This passage refers to rest from the burdens of the world and the yoke of sin that occurs when we commit ourselves to Christ. Still, it is important to note that Jesus is the source of lasting rest, so coming into His presence in worship and prayer is a powerful means of rest. Also, Jesus tells us His burden is light, meaning that a thriving, learning relationship with our Lord can take away life's worries and weariness.

In looking at the Bible, rest, like work, has spiritual value. It is a godly activity, for God rested even though it was not necessary for Him to do so. Rest allows us to take our nose away from the grindstone and gain insight and perspective regarding our efforts. It enables us to focus total attention on God in worship and prayer. Thus, a regular dose of rest after a busy week is certainly nothing to feel guilty about.

Then why do we feel guilty about rest? Why can't we seem to find time for it in our schedules? Each of us may have answers to those questions, but the problem is inherent in our culture. According to Robert Banks in *The Tyranny of Time*, our occupation with busyness began with the Enlightenment of the eighteenth century, when life became increasingly secularized. Without an eternal perspective, life on earth became everything:

> The more people confined their sights to the material and temporal horizons of this world, the stronger the temptation to realise [sic] all their goals, and find all their values, within this world. Their desire for immediate gains placed a growing pressure upon the time at their disposal. A more intensive use of everyday time and a stronger belief in human progress eventuated. [3]

The progression of this non-Christian thinking eventually transformed our views toward rest, particularly with the rise of utilitarianism in the late nineteenth century. Banks writes:

> Utilitarian attitudes began to affect people's attitude to their free time. The view gradually prevailed that only useful activity was valuable, moral and meaningful. Unless their rest and recreation achieved something "worthwhile," people felt guilty. Relaxation as an end in itself, pure play and idleness all came under censure or suspicion. The hobby, competitive games and leisure activities started to supplant them. [4]

As Christians, it is important to realize the source of our busyness and problems with rest. Society has sped up only as Christianity lost its influence. Unfortunately, instead of showing the world a better way, we usually try to keep up with or even lead the pack. Instead of developing a more Christlike character, we often substitute a flurry of activity of only marginal heavenly significance.

"Just Do It" has become more than a catchy sneaker slogan; it has become a rallying cry for the philosophy of the day. Don't think about it, don't pray about it, don't weigh the consequences of potential actions, just go out there and do something, anything, everything. No wonder everybody's tired!

How to Find Rest

How do we break the endless cycle of work addiction and find rest? Here are a few suggestions.

1. Understand that rest is not spare time; it must be scheduled regularly. Take a minute right now to glance at your calendar or planner. If you're like most of us, it is filled with appointments, work tasks, and social obligations. Have you ever penciled in time for rest?

> **Our Heavenly Father doesn't have a finish-your-homework rule.**

Most of us don't set aside time for rest. We still remember our childhood, when our parents would only let us go out and play after we finished all our homework. As adults, however, the "homework" is never totally finished. We need to understand, writes Gordon MacDonald, that our Heavenly Father doesn't have a finish-your-homework rule:

> We do not rest because our work is done; we rest because God commanded it and created us to have a need for it....Most of us think of resting as something we do *after* our work is done. But Sabbath is not something that happens after. It may in fact be something that is pursued *before*. If we assume that this rest comes only after work is complete, many of us are in trouble, for we have jobs where the work is never finished. And that in part is why some of us rarely rest; never finishing our work, we do not think to take the time for Sabbath peace and restoration. [5]

This week, try inserting some time for rest in your calendar. Perhaps you can set aside a few hours on Sunday afternoon or Saturday morning or some evening. My personal recommendation would be to start your time with a brief prayer, spending some quiet time thinking. Now you shouldn't be thinking about all the stuff you ought to be doing right then. Reflect back on the past week and think about your goals for the weeks ahead. If you don't like just sitting, try a quiet walk around the neighborhood or a nearby park.

Sometimes you'll need to show restraint in your work schedule to allow time for rest. Jerry Dettinger easily could have worked long hours in building his fitness equipment business, especially since he loved the work. Yet he decided early on to limit his job to between 45 and 50 hours a week so he could live a more balanced life.

A balanced life complete with adequate rest might even improve your performance at the office. Lord Chesterfield once said, "Few people do business well who do nothing else."

2. Give your relationship to God first priority in your life and your schedule. Have you ever been with a manager who said quality was the top priority in the company, yet he spends most of his time cutting costs and shredding budgets? In his books, Tom Peters stresses the importance of having one's calendar reflect the area of greatest importance to the company. The walk needs to match the talk.

At times, I feel as if my walk doesn't match my talk in spiritual matters. I call Jesus my Lord, yet too often I don't seem to find much time for Him, squeezing in a quick prayer at the end of the day. My intentions are good, but urgent matters tend to crowd God out of my schedule.

A minimal expectation for our relationship with God is time for quality worship, both on Sunday and alone during the week. Worship helps put God back on the throne in our hearts and can provide a rest deeper than sleep or relaxation alone.

I have a friend attending graduate school who occasionally has a debate with his wife on Sunday mornings. Both want rest, but one wants to sleep in while the other wishes to worship in church. Having slept in a few Sunday mornings in my youth, I know that worship provides far more lasting rest. Josef Pieper once said, "Cut off from the worship of the divine, leisure becomes laziness and work inhuman." [6]

Next on our schedule should be a daily time of prayer and Scripture study. As I've mentioned before, prayer is perhaps the single most important activity we can undertake to make our work an effective ministry. It also takes away feelings of anxiety and extreme fatigue. I don't know how God does it but, no matter how rushed and overwhelmed I am, when I take time to come to Him, those feelings disappear.

How much time should we give God? There is no set formula; besides, we can offer short prayers up to God throughout the day. I learned to pray from a little booklet called "7 Minutes With God." The guide was meant to provide a starting point for new believers, but for years I rarely prayed much longer than that. A big breakthrough came when my schedule changed, so I would have two days a week to write full-time. For those days, I made a commitment to spend an hour in prayer before I would try to write a single word. I cannot adequately describe the difference those hours have meant in my relationship with God and in my work. Now the goal is to extend my commitment to the other five days of the week.

To grow in Christ, we need to give Him at least as much attention as our significant human relationships. Imagine how foolish it would be to attempt a seven-minute date. Or to conduct a quickie job interview. God desires and deserves a deeper relationship.

3. *Periodically review why you do what you do.* Top companies always set aside time to rethink their purpose, priorities, and plans. Each Christian needs to do the same. Without a strong sense of purpose and priorities, we tend to take on any worthy project that comes our way. Without a plan, we fail to get done today the things we need to do to be better prepared for future tasks. We end up busy but off-target.

> **Without a strong sense of purpose and priorities, we tend to take on any worthy project that comes our way.**

For me, I need to schedule at least a day each year to get away and review my life in God's presence. Almost every major insight or change in my life's direction came about during those times. I recommitted my life to Christ during a quiet Fourth of July at home alone; I decided to write for God instead of the best-seller charts during a winter's hike in the woods near Lake Superior; my decision to teach and write about work came after a three-day silent retreat.

If you've never spent time thinking about your purpose, priorities, and plans, I recommend setting aside at least two days for the process. The details of such a retreat will vary, depending on what issues you are currently facing. In most instances, you can adapt business planning techniques you may be familiar with, along with some reflection from Scripture. One passage you might use to reflect on is Matthew 6:19-21. Think about what kind of heavenly treasures you'd like to create during your lifetime. Thus far in your life, what would God point to and say, "Well done, good and faithful servant"?

4. *Try to simplify your material life.* Despite all the "labor-saving" devices invented in recent years, I agree with Banks and others who claim that an affluent lifestyle brings about impoverishment in terms of time:

> While we take pleasure in the wider range of goods we can have, we need more time to enjoy them all. Since the marginal increases in free time that have come our way are nowhere near large enough to cope with the range of goods we have acquired, our free time becomes more pressured. In order to

enjoy all our possessions we have to maximise [*sic*] use of our leisure time. One way we do this is by consuming several things at once! It is not uncommon to find someone attempting to listen to the stereo, read the newspaper and eat a meal all at one time. Leisure time is scheduled like a working day so that as many hard-earned consumer goods as possible can be sampled.[7]

One of the most significant "time-wasters" in most people's lives is time spent acquiring, using, and maintaining material possessions. A large house full of gadgets and toys is a much larger drain on one's time than a simpler dwelling and fewer possessions. I learned this lesson from my mother when my parents visited me some years back. While my father was off at a business meeting, I took Mom on a walk around a beautiful lake, surrounded by some of the most stately old homes in the city. Mother was not impressed. Every time I pointed out a particularly striking mansion, she responded, "Boy, I'd hate to clean that house!"

Of course, I tried to explain to her that these owners probably didn't clean their own homes—but I had missed her point. More stuff and bigger houses mean more work and less time for rest and other more meaningful pursuits of life.

One way to simplify our material life is to put limits on what we buy. Without constraints, most of us purchase more than we need and spend all the money we have. Not too many years ago, close friends sometimes called me "Mr. Mail Order" because most of the clothing, books, and musical recordings I owned came via mail-order catalogues. Some weeks, I spent hours thumbing through the pages of glossy photos to assemble my orders.

It was when I set strict annual budgets for myself in those three buying categories that I started to break the shopping habit. Why flip through an 80-page catalogue when my clothing budget is stretched to the limit? Putting limits on my spending ended up saving me both time and money. As a bonus, I don't get as much junk mail anymore.

5. *Simplify your non-work life.* People suffering from work addiction can abuse what little free time they have in two ways. First, they can make work of leisure activities. We don't exercise; we "work" out. We don't play games or sports for fun; we compete to win. In time, everything becomes work.

Several years after becoming a Christian, Kathy gave up playing in racquetball tournaments. She had been one of the top amateur players in the state, amassing shelves of trophies. But then her need to compete lessened, so she no longer desired to spend entire weekends at tournaments. Instead, she continued to play the game frequently—for fun.

The other way of abusing free time is to squander it without gaining rest. In our culture television is the worst offender. For many families, half the available leisure time is spent staring at the TV screen. Every once in awhile, something entertaining or informative is put on the air. Usually, we complain about how awful television is, yet we still invest the equivalent of a day or two of full-time work watching it.

One of the smartest things Kathy and I ever did was to give up television for a week. (It was her idea.) Instead of watching sitcoms during supper, we talked. Instead of leaving the TV on after dinner, we both found better ways to occupy our time. For me, it was the most productive and restful week I've ever had. We haven't quit watching TV altogether, but it has become a much smaller part of our lives.

Give genuine rest a try. You'll likely discover, as I have, that rested people often get more done than if they had just toiled away every day of the week. And they stand out like shining stars in today's hurried, harried workforce.

Think about It

❑ If you keep a detailed calendar of your activities, go back and look through the last few weeks. Was rest or time with God scheduled for any time slots? If you are tired and feel as if you are not spending enough time with God, go to next week's schedule and block off some time for this before you schedule other obligations.

❑ When was the last time you set aside a day just to spend with God? Consider planning such a day.

Notes

1. "Roper's America," *Adweek's Marketing Week* (29 July 1991): 11.

2. Doug Sherman and William Hendricks, *Keeping Your Ethical Edge Sharp* (Colorado Springs: NavPress, 1990), 195.

3. Robert Banks, *The Tyranny of Time* (Downers Grove, Ill.: InterVarsity Press, 1983), 109-10.

4. Ibid., 111.

5. Gordon MacDonald, *Ordering Your Private World* (Nashville: Oliver-Nelson Books, 1984), 187-88.

6. Josef Pieper, as quoted in Leland Ryken, *Work & Leisure in Christian Perspective* (Portland, Ore.: Multnomah Press, 1987), 204.

7. Banks, *The Tyranny of Time*, 123

13

Entrepreneurs As Ministry Leaders

··

Perhaps you've always had a dream of owning a business some-day. Or maybe while reading the previous chapters, you've fre-quently thought or said, "That would never fly where I work."

Although God can provide for us great ministry potential in virtu-ally every work situation, I still believe the entrepreneurial option is worth prayerful consideration. Say, for example, you hold a middle management position in a hopelessly misguided chain of gift shops. How would things be different if you ran the company? Think of the loving workplace you could create; think of all those previously disgruntled customers you could win over. If you're doubtful about your prospects of ever leading the company or having much influence over its direction, you might want to consider someday opening a shop of your own.

> **How would things be different if you ran the company?**

Why Entrepreneurism?

Why the emphasis on launching a business? Well, for starters, entre-preneurism may be the only legitimate avenue available for those seeking leadership positions. The traditional mode of ascending the corporate ladder is more difficult today for two reasons: the down-sizing of corporate staffs and the age demographics of executives. According to one estimate, the turn of the century will see such a glut of white collar Baby Boomers that there will be at least twenty highly-qualified candidates for every single upper-level position in corporate America. [1]

While larger corporations get leaner and meaner, each week thousands of new enterprises are launched. Part of the allure of entrepreneurism is its freedom, especially the freedom from all the bureaucratic twists and quirks of big business.

Is this freedom desirable? In earlier chapters, we drew wisdom from the instruction of Paul and Peter to slaves, since those workers share some commonalities with today's wage earners. Although Paul tells slaves that in their toil they are serving Christ (Col. 3:24), he does not discourage them from seeking their freedom: "Were you a slave when you were called? Don't let it trouble you—although if you can gain your freedom, do so" (1 Cor. 7:21).

So, despite the inherent spiritual value present in all our business work, there are several reasons for Christians to remain open to the prospect of starting up or heading up a company.

1. Top leaders greatly determine the values and culture of their organizations. If you want to know why certain companies are more prone to treating their customers like kings and queens, making their employees feel like they count—in short, making the world a little bit better—look to the top. Organizations have always drawn their vision and values from their leaders. They inspire change, set limits, and determine company priorities.

Strong business leaders can leave a mark on their organizations that can far outlive their service. Ford Motors still bears the strong imprint of Henry Ford and his family. The same impact can be seen at Wal-Mart (Sam Walton), Apple (Steve Jobs), IBM (Tom Watson, Sr.) and McDonald's

> **Strong business leaders can leave a mark on their organizations that can far outlive their service.**

(Ray Kroc). In fact, writes Lawrence Miller, one of the greatest acts of leadership is to pass on one's values to the next generation:

> What higher achievement by a manager can there be than to leave to posterity others who have adopted his spirit of integrity and purpose? If only every manager could be aware

of his or her potential influence on future generations if he or she took the time to nuture others.... Perhaps the most important management-development task that our corporations face is to create a cultural learning process that teaches young managers to act on superior belief systems, to do that which they know to be right, according to a higher standard than what seems most expedient. [2]

The vision and values of a leader can last for many years, particularly if they are easily understood and widely communicated. At Johnson & Johnson, Robert Wood Johnson wrote a document called "Our Credo," back in 1947. In it he set the company's priorities. Their first responsibility was to the doctors, nurses, and patients who used their products. Next came employees and then their communities, including the "community of man." Last came the shareholders because Johnson believed they would always be well served if the company held to these principles.

The credibility of the Credo was tested 35 years later, when someone laced Johnson & Johnson's Tylenol capsules with cyanide, which killed six people and frightened a nation. The company won public praise by its swift and decisive action, recalling 31 million bottles of the pain reliever at a cost of $100 million.

James E. Burke, Johnson & Johnson's Chairman and CEO at the time, said the Credo played the most important role in their decision-making during the Tylenol tragedy. With customers who depend on their products as their top responsibility, what other decision could have been made? "We resolved to do everything that is right," said Burke. "And if my company did everything that was right, the Lord would make it come out right." [3]

2. Leading a business is a great opportunity to serve others. When you head up a company, you have the power and the potential to serve customers and create a loving environment for your employees, the focus of chapters 6 and 7. Although most businesses give these concepts no more than mere lip service, the company you lead can be different.

Service means to "put other people's needs ahead of yours," says Mike Olson, who heads up a financial services agency. He believes that to say it but not do it is being dishonest. In his own business, to "do it" has sometimes meant turning away business, telling certain people "you can't afford to do business with us."

Besides serving customers, employees provide endless potential for service every day of the year. As you start or grow a business, the creation of good new jobs represents a great blessing, particularly for the families of those who fill them. Also, through your vision, values, and treatment of people, you can add meaning to the lives of your workers. According to Lawrence Miller, the current lack of meaning is one of the weaknesses in business today:

> The search for meaning and significance is a central characteristic of the human soul. Every person would like to find meaning and significance in his or her work. How many corporations provide this opportunity? The degree to which an organization is perceived to be in pursuit of and is acting consistent with noble ideals is the degree to which it is possible for the individual to believe that his or her efforts on behalf of the organization will be personally meaningful and significant. It is this spiritual deficiency in the culture of our corporations that we must address.[4]

Who better to address that spiritual deficiency than Christians? Filled with the love of Christ, who could create a more loving and nurturing work environment than His followers? I remember a comment made at an outreach luncheon by Rose Totino, cofounder of Totino's Pizza. She said accepting Christ changed her entire business outlook. "I loved everybody and everybody loved working for us. It was just a great, great experience."

3. *Top business leaders are highly visible witnesses.* Heads of companies witness to the world both individually, as high-profile business leaders, and corporately, as their beliefs are reflected in the practices of their firms. Running a business is much like taking an oral examination in front of an audience; everyone knows when you are right and wrong. No other endeavor tests and reveals character more than business, writes Paul Hawken:

> The moment you enter the world of business—as a provider, not merely as a consumer—you will have a hundred opportu-

nities a day to act beneficially or wrongly, to deal with people fairly or otherwise, to enhance your social environment or pollute it. Imagine your favorite store in which the people are kind and responsive. Imagine the opposite store. Now imagine your own store or warehouse or factory. Every business presents the same choices.

> **Filled with the love of Christ, who could create a more loving and nurturing work environment than His followers?**

Besides being visible witnesses, top leaders—particularly business owners—sometimes have greater flexibility in responding to other ministry needs. According to Jim Bever, being an entrepreneur is "a perfect opportunity to have a ministry, because you can call your own destination and you're in charge of your own time." Bever uses that flexibility to spend time discipling other men and going on short-term mission trips during his winter slow season.

4. Being in charge allows you to create a position which maximizes the use of your abilities and interests. In chapter 5, we discussed the importance of discovering our vocational calling, as well as the difficulties in finding job openings that fit our gifts and interests. In starting a business, you create your own job, so there will be only one person to blame if it doesn't suit you.

If you can't talk passionately about a particular product or service, don't even consider starting up a business in that field. According to Jerry Dettinger, entrepreneurs should always operate in areas that interest them, which, in his own case, was exercise and fitness. "Go get paid for what cranks you up," he said.

Your Business Is God's Tool

For the committed Christian, a business enterprise can be a powerful tool to reach the world for Jesus. Sometimes God will use the business for more tangible, physical ministry purposes, such as making people healthier or cleaning up Earth's waters. Other times he will use the venture to meet deeper needs, paving the way to

175

reach the deepest need of all: the empty void in the lives of those who do not know Christ.

For me, those are pretty powerful reasons to consider starting up a business.

Think about It

❑ Have you ever thought to yourself, *Someday I'd like to run my own business or I could run this company better than its current leaders?* Consider spending some time exploring your entrepreneurial options and seeking God's guidance.

Notes

1. Thomas F. Jones, *Entrepreneurism: The Mythical, the True and the New* (New York: Donald I. Fine, Inc., 1987), 20.

2. Lawrence M. Miller, *American Spirit: Visions of a New Corporate Culture* (New York: William Morrow & Company, Inc., 1984), 132–33.

3. Fred Reed, "Living Under Authority Means Acting Accordingly in Deeds, Not Just Words," *Spiritual Fitness in Business,* (January 1986): 2-3.

4. Lawrence Miller, *American Spirit,* 19.

5. Paul Hawken, *Growing a Business* (New York: Simon and Schuster, 1987), 28.

14

Sharing Your Time
and Your Faith

···

A s you come to the final chapters of this book, I wonder if some of you may be thinking: *It's about time we get to what's really important, like witnessing and evangelism.* Perhaps a few of you skipped ahead to these pages, a little disappointed that I devoted only one chapter to workplace evangelism. Don't be disappointed. We've been concentrating on improving our witness all along. Just as we know that ministry is not limited to what goes on in churches, evangelism is far more than handing out tracts and getting people to pray to receive Jesus. Taking this limited view of evangelism tends to cause us to discount our worth as missionaries. This is wrong thinking, according to Pastor Bill Hybels:

> I am always disappointed to hear sincere Christians say that if they had their lives to live over again, they would be foreign missionaries so that they could really serve the Lord! The Bible teaches repeatedly that we are *all* missionaries, no matter where we are. We are missionaries to our families, to our neighbors, and to the world of people we rub shoulders with in the marketplace. By how we work, who we are, and what we say, we can bring a Christian influence to our jobsite that can have far-reaching effects in the lives of men and women who desperately need to hear of God's forgiveness, and we can bring honor and glory to the name of our Lord. [1]

Hybels clearly and simply identifies the three key aspects of our

177

workplace evangelism efforts: how we work, who we are, what we say. Let's take a closer look at each element.

How We Work

A large portion of this book has dealt with how we work, simply because it is what those in the marketplace see the most. Non-Christians can learn much about God from watching the mature Christian labor.

❏ By committing our activities to God, others witness the power of our Lord at work.

❏ As we discover and develop our God-given gifts, we confront non-Christians as someone with a sense of calling, aware of our proper place in this world.

❏ As we serve others around us—customers, superiors, employees—we spread around the love of Christ the servant.

❏ By acting with honesty and integrity, others will notice that our morals have a deeper foundation than our society's expedient "values."

What we do during the daily grind has great eternal consequences. This is why slaves and other workers are repeatedly urged to be careful in how they work and live. In 1 Timothy 6:1, those under the yoke of slavery are told to "consider their masters worthy of full respect, so that God's name and our teaching may not be slandered." Wrong actions can undermine right teachings.

Right actions, however, can enhance the reception of God's teaching. Slaves are told in Titus 2:9-10 to show their masters that they can be fully trusted, "so that in every way they will make the teaching about God our Savior attractive." In 1 Thessalonians 4:11-12, Paul instructs believers to lead a quiet life of work, "so that your daily life may win the respect of outsiders." It is important for

Christians to be "very careful" in how we live, in order to make "the most of every opportunity" (Eph. 5:15-16).

Even a mundane task such as dealing with vendors can become a great opportunity. Years ago, the Billy Graham Evangelistic Association called up a fledgling public relations professional to give him a large project. The man had lost his job and was struggling to start his own PR business. At the conclusion of the project, his contact at Billy Graham asked him to deliver his bill in person. And he was given a check on the spot. For the next several years, this Christian organization continued to monitor the progress of the man's business, providing additional projects for him along the way. Only later did he realize that their main motive was to help him get his business off the ground. He has sent them a sizable donation every year since.

As a result of honorably working with vendors, BGEA gained a new donor. Also, Harvey Mackay, another Billy Graham vendor, took an entire chapter to retell the story in his mega-best-seller, *Swim with the Sharks Without Being Eaten Alive.* This ministry earned high praise and respect from two Jewish men, not through an outreach event, but through how they conducted their business affairs.

Who We Are

Although who we are is reflected in our work, it goes beyond those actions. Anyone is capable of doing good works. Only Christians can portray Christ's love and character to the world. Others see His strength when we stand strong under terrible adversity. They see His compassion when we reach out in love to those who are hurting. And they see His character when we are willing to go against the flow, to stand firm for a truth which is absolute.

We are more than mere doers of the Word or sayers of the Word. We are "the light of the world" (Matt. 5:14). We who "shine like stars in the universe" (Phil. 2:15) are God's intended tool for pushing back the darkness in our world. As we grow in our faith and become more Christlike, God uses us as a powerful lighthouse beacon to help bring the lost closer to Him.

Although, as Christians, we place great emphasis on telling others about Jesus, it is who we are that determines whether they'll listen. A Christian, known for bringing many to Christ in a place where public evangelism is taboo, was asked how he did it. He responded, "I love them until they ask why!"

What We Say

What we say to others is important, but sometimes what God wants us to share and what we think we ought to share are different. The evangelistic techniques I was exposed to in my youth seem strikingly similar to the now outdated "hard sell" approach in business sales. Success was determined by the number of prospects you called on (the number of people you told about Jesus) and the number of times you attempted to "close" the sale (asked them to pray to receive Jesus). Although this approach has many followers and does work with some people, I think these New Testament verses suggest a different emphasis:

> Be wise in the way you act toward outsiders; make the most of every opportunity. Let your conversation be always full of grace, seasoned with salt, so that you may know how to answer everyone (Col. 4:5-6).
> But in your hearts set apart Christ as Lord. Always be prepared to give an answer to everyone who asks you to give the reason for the hope that you have (1 Peter 3:15).

We are not to corner and assault people with the Gospel, but to "season" our conversation.

These passages are crammed with wisdom. First, note again the importance of our actions. Being wise in how we act toward outsiders is a key to making the most of the opportunities God provides us. We are not to corner and assault people with the Gospel, but to "season" our conversation. Also, both passages use the term "answer" when referring to sharing our faith. When people clearly see a difference in our lives, they will want to know why.

What if no one is asking about the hope that is within us? If no one seems interested in listening to us talk about Jesus, the temptation is to focus on what we can say to create more interest or be more persuasive. In business, that would be the equivalent of just tweaking the advertising to resuscitate a failed product. So instead of focusing on making our lives a better witness, we concentrate on getting better at selling the Gospel. That is a mistake, according to Doug Sherman and William Hendricks:

> ...too many Christians have given the gospel a bad reputation by their crude, insensitive, soapbox approach to evangelism. What's worse, many do it without a lifestyle and workstyle to back it up. The order is terribly important! If you want to win a hearing for the gospel, start by being the best worker you can be, and gain the respect of your peers. Match that workstyle with a lifestyle so unique and distinctive that your coworkers will want to know why. If that happens, you'll have plenty of opportunities to discuss your faith. And when you do, you'll find yourself having a powerful impact on others. [2]

Part of a Vast Missionary Army

Getting it right in how we work, who we are, and what we say is of critical importance. For we are not just people at work. We are part of God's largest missionary army, an army stationed at the most strategic location in our culture: the marketplace.

As I mentioned earlier, lack of cohesion in our neighborhoods and increasing numbers of unchurched people mean that workplaces are the most significant "communities" to which most Americans belong. It so dominates our culture that Sherman and Hendricks have labeled it

If Christians desire to turn our nation around and lead it to the Lord, then the workplace must be a significant priority for ministry.

"the distribution point for change." [3] In other words, if Christians desire to turn our nation around and lead it to the Lord, then the workplace must be a significant priority for ministry.

That is good news because the workplace is where most Christians are already serving. Frank Tillapaugh, in *Unleashing the Church*, describes the vast potential of this ministry team:

The on-the-job Christian is the largest potential missionary force available to the church. It exists with international possibilities as well as with inner-city influence. There is no strata of society, no technical skill, no professional language into which the Christian community has not already penetrated. The task is to mobilize, train, and encourage that missionary force so that it can see, evangelize, and disciple as the apostle Paul did in his tentmaking activities in Corinth. [4]

Despite those days when it seems as if we're going it alone in our Christian walk, we are part of a large army in the marketplace. At this time, however, we are not an organized force. Most of us soldiers are only vaguely aware of our duties and have not spent much time getting trained and equipped. Our leadership is difficult to distinguish and communication between troops is poor. We soldiers often feel trapped behind enemy lines, hardly ready to take the offensive.

Despite its problems, this marketplace army is too huge to dismiss. Besides, the needs in our society are far too extensive to be met by those we traditionally have considered "ministers." The task requires God's use of the whole body of Christ, for our Savior's words in Matthew 9:37-38 still hold true today: "The harvest is plentiful but the workers are few. Ask the Lord of the harvest, therefore, to send out workers into His harvest field."

Where is the harvest? Most of us don't have to look very far to find unhappy souls in desperate need of the Son of God.

❏ A coworker down the hall from you is obsessed with "getting ahead" no matter the cost. She will shade the truth or deceive people in order to impress those above her in the organization. Her world revolves around the trappings of success—an executive home, trendy cars, a prestigious title—and she can't understand why people waste their time with religion.

❏ Your company's newest employee, an older man, doesn't seem to fit in with the others. He's struggling in his efforts to catch on to all the work routines, but no one offers to help him—and he's too shy to ask. With each passing day, his expression grows more frustrated and hopeless.

❑ Down the hall, another manager's mother recently passed away. Their relationship was very close, so the loss has left her visibly shaken. She's angry and hurt that her mother had to go during a time when she was still trying to get over her miscarriage.

❑ Your next-door neighbor has lost his job after working for the same corporation for over twenty years. He took such great pride in his work and the success of his employer that now he looks like a lost puppy. The job search has not gone well, either.

Yes, there is the potential for a great harvest out in the marketplace, and God intends to use those of us already working in the field. Christ commissions us to "go and make disciples of all nations" in Matthew 28:19. He also gives us the power to be effective witnesses in two forms: the Holy Spirit (Acts 1:8) and the Gospel itself (Rom. 1:16).

Ways to Strengthen Our Witness

To be a part of God's harvest requires us to continually evaluate and fine-tune our witness to others. Besides conducting our business affairs according to Christ's servant approach (portrayed throughout this book), here are a few more ideas to help strengthen our witness.

1. Develop a heart for the lost souls around you. As we live each day, it is important to see the world through the compassionate eyes of Jesus. We've read Christ's statement that the harvest is plentiful, but let's look at the situation in Matthew 9:35-38 that led to His comment:

> Jesus went through all the towns and villages, teaching in their synagogues, preaching the good news of the kingdom and healing every disease and sickness. When He saw the crowds, He had compassion on them, because they were harassed and helpless, like sheep without a shepherd. Then He said to His disciples, "The harvest is plentiful but the workers are few. Ask the Lord of the harvest, therefore, to send workers into His harvest field."

God saw the lost and sent them a shepherd, Jesus, to guide the way. Because of His compassion for the lost, Christ sends us out as His workers, to show people the way back to Him. Instead of looking at the people around us and expressing disgust at their sins—adultery, profanity, greed, envy, lust—we need to see them as people unwittingly about to step off a cliff. In fact, we'd all be better witnesses if we spent some time pondering the fate of the non-Christians we know, pondering to the point of genuine grief. Perhaps then we would overcome our inhibitions and reach out in love to gently guide them out of harm's way.

> **We'd all be better witnesses if we spent some time pondering the fate of the non-Christians we know, pondering to the point of genuine grief.**

Walt Meloon clearly remembered the grief he and his brother faced when their business went through bankruptcy proceedings years ago. As cofounder of Correct Craft, a boat-building firm in Orlando, Florida, Walt felt a deep desire to help others in dire business situations. He provided leadership in starting Turnaround Ministries, whose Turnaround Weekends—an all-expenses-paid retreat of fellowship and encouragement for business couples facing bankruptcy—are credited for having saved a number of marriages, in addition to the spiritual turnarounds.

2. Be there for others. Former Bethlehem Steel executive William Diehl calls this act "the ministry of presence." [5] If we don't spend time with people, listen to their problems, and just hang out with them, our opportunities for ministry are limited. For those of you who work with a wild crowd, "hanging out" may take you to establishments your pastor wouldn't likely book for the church banquet. Although being there for others should not lead us into sin, we need to remember the example of Jesus. He did not bring people into "church" to get saved; He went to them.

One of my early business friends was a heavy drinker and womanizer, which meant a bar was his place of choice for socializing. Despite his bad habits, I enjoyed his company. Because of our friendship, I ate lots of happy hour food, helped him on moving day, discussed spiritual matters when they came up, and prayed for him.

I praise God that, several years later, he accepted Christ. However, I have needed to ask forgiveness for when I "haven't had enough time" for the many other people who have come into my life.

3. *Pray for those with whom you work.* This is not the first time in these pages I have advocated prayer—and it won't be the last. Prayer is not merely something we do to make our ministry efforts more effective; it is the foundational element of our actual ministry to others. The best single action we can take for others is to pray regularly for them.

One approach I've found helpful is to make an exhaustive list of all the people with whom I interact most frequently, plus any other names I wish to add. Although they are in the minority, Christians are included on the list because they need prayer support in their own ministry efforts. My goal is to pray through the entire list at least once a week.

How should we pray for non-Christians? For starters, pray for their salvation and any other needs they have in their lives. Also, ask God to let you know whether you are to be part of His answer to those prayers. For people you see frequently or are close to, expect God to use you in some capacity. Pray for opportunities to get to know them better, to help them in their struggles, to show God's love through your actions and testimony.

A coworker of mine has endured years of severe family health struggles. One day she asked me to pray for her. I told her that I had been praying for her and would continue. "Pray harder," she replied with a smile. Every few months, she continues to hold me accountable in that way.

4. *Wait for the Holy Spirit's leading.* Understanding God's timing is important because *we* don't actually lead people to Christ, the Holy Spirit does. Unless the Holy Spirit is working in people's hearts already, they will not accept the Gospel message, no matter how well we deliver it. First

> **Instead of just randomly sharing the Gospel (with most of our words falling on deaf ears), a wiser approach is to see where God is at work and join Him.**

Corinthians 2:14 states that one "without the Spirit" will neither accept nor understand things coming from God. According to 2 Corinthians 4:4, the mind of unbelievers has been blinded, "so that they cannot see the light of the Gospel."

So what do we do then? Instead of just randomly sharing the Gospel (with most of our words falling on deaf ears), a wiser approach is to see where God is at work and join Him. In *Experiencing God*, Henry Blackaby and Claude King claim that we can clearly discern God's work in others:

No one will seek God or pursue spiritual things unless the Spirit of God is at work in his life. Suppose a neighbor, a friend, or one of your children begins to inquire after spiritual things. You do not have to question whether that is God drawing him or her. He is the only one who can do that. No one will ever seek after God unless God is at work in his life. Many people who have begun applying this understanding to their witnessing have found great freedom. They pray and watch to see how God is working in the lives of others. When they see or hear someone seeking after God, that becomes their invitation to bear witness to the God they know and serve. [6]

When people become receptive to God, they will give a number of "buying signals," says Jeff Hagen, area director for Search Ministries. "They will include you in their social calendar, show an interest in spiritual things, ask questions, and open their lives up to you." Giving them an opportunity to talk about spiritual matters is critical to bringing them closer to the Lord.

During a class I took on the ministry of the laity, I learned of the concept of being a "reluctant witness." At first it sounded like pure heresy. After all, we're supposed to share the Gospel whenever we can, right? Well, we are instructed to make disciples, but the fact of the matter is that no one comes to the Lord Jesus unless the Father draws him in (John 6:44). Being a reluctant witness involves waiting on the Lord, restraining our tongue until we see the Holy Spirit at work in the other person and feel the Spirit's nudge within our own heart.

As many of you know, the nudge of the Holy Spirit is very clear. In my own case, the knot in my stomach is a sign that God wants me to do something that does not come naturally for me. I know of one man who couldn't sleep at night because he felt God wanted him to share the Gospel with his boss. The man obeyed and his boss accepted the Lord.

5. Accept others as they are. Remember the old saying, "hate the sin, love the sinner"? It's a saying we need to keep in mind as we form relationships with non-Christians. Quite often our feelings for others are colored by the sins they commit, causing us to despise them or try to convince them to give up their bad habits. Either way, we will be hindered in forming a close, open relationship with them.

Strategically, trying to coax non-Christians away from their major sins is like trying to convince a bear and a trout to become friends. Everything in the bear's nature says to eat the fish, while the trout's natural response is to swim away quickly. Changing habits is next to impossible without a change in the person first.

> **Strategically, trying to coax non-Christians away from their major sins is like trying to convince a bear and a trout to become friends.**

The medical profession knows it is ultimately futile to treat the symptoms of an illness unless the cause of the problem is discovered and corrected. For non-Christians, the sinful life is but a symptom of being separated from God. If a person is promiscuous, will trying to convince him to settle for one partner get him to heaven? No. Only accepting Jesus will accomplish that. Moreover, without the power of the Holy Spirit, will that person have the strength to stop sleeping around? Not likely.

Our job in the world is not that of moral police officer but that of an ambassador of God's love. In 1 Corinthians 5:9-13, Paul writes that although we have a right to judge and rebuke those within the church, God alone is to judge outsiders. We must love them with Christ's unconditional love and encourage them each step they take closer to God.

Don't give up on "big" sinners. On my prayer list, the first person to accept Jesus was probably the "biggest" sinner of the bunch. God is able to love him despite all the terrible things he did before—and so should I.

6. Be prepared to tell your story. Sharing the Gospel does not require learning to preach a rousing sermon or share hundreds of Bible passages from memory with great precision.

First Peter 3:15 tells us, "Always be prepared to give an answer to everyone who asks you to give the reason for the hope that you have." If your life has been a good witness to others, what they desire most is to hear your story, not some fine-sounding sermon.

I believe the best way to be prepared to give an answer is to write out your personal testimony, at least in outline form. Include how you came to the Lord and how He makes a difference in your life. Be as specific as possible. For coworkers, you might want to share how your relationship with Christ affects how you work and treat others. Your testimony doesn't need to be dramatic to be effective, just honest and real.

Although you will never read your testimony to another person, writing it out is useful for two reasons. First, it allows you to think through your story and organize it logically. Second, having written out your testimony will enable you to remember its key points better at the moment of truth: when you share it with someone else.

Another useful way to be prepared for sharing is to have some knowledge of key Scripture verses relating to salvation which, for starters, include Proverbs 14:12, Isaiah 59:2, John 1:12, 3:16, Romans 3:23, 5:8, 6:23, 10:9, 10:13, Ephesians 2:8-9, 1 Timothy 2:5, 1 John 5:12-13, and Revelation 3:20. It might also be helpful to keep a supply of tracts on hand that outline the process of coming to know Christ. In my own case, I almost always have within my reach a copy of "Steps to Peace with God," published by the Billy Graham Evangelistic Association. I don't hand it out blindly, but I use it as a visual aid in discussing the way to salvation. Also, giving a person something to read later may prove helpful in his or her moment of decision.

7. Leave the results in God's hands. Too often we have a seller's attitude toward evangelism. Our only focus is to close the sale, get a person to make the decision, pray the prayer, and be done with it. Even though the decision point is important, the process of making disciples takes much longer.

For those of you who have a garden, let's use Christ's harvest analogy. Although harvesting a garden is important, many tasks must be performed before and after the harvest to attain a good yield: tilling, planting, cultivation, watering, weeding, crop cleaning, and storage. I must admit that harvesting is my favorite part of gardening, so much so that I am slow to take on some of the other chores. Without Kathy's help in planting, watering, and weeding, my harvest would be pretty puny.

Evangelism is not just an event or a decision but a process. As participants, our goal should be to let God use us to bring people one step closer to Him. Our roles will be different, depending on where the person is when we meet him or her. In one case, we may be plowing rocky ground; in another, watering the seeds someone else has planted. Sometimes, we'll have the privilege of being there at harvest time. The key to effective evangelism is that we are all out working in the garden and being obedient to the projects God gives us.

8. Be part of a small group of Christians for support. Sometimes the most important part of our ministry efforts is realizing we are not alone. Being a member of the body of Christ means we don't have to singlehandedly win our company over for Jesus. When we share and pray with other Christians, we can begin to feel like we're part of the army of God, ready to do battle again.

If you are not already part of a small group, I strongly recommend that you join one or start one. Words cannot capture the value I've found in having loving Christians who will pray for my needs and those people I seek to reach—as well as offer me encouragement and accountability. As a bonus, I get to see God answer the prayers of others, with their triumphs giving me hope during times when I am struggling.

Small groups can exist in an almost infinite variety of forms and settings.

❏ Many churches are forming small groups, sometimes called cell groups, to provide the intimate relationships and personal ministry that can't otherwise be provided, particularly in larger churches.

❏ Ministry groups like Christian Business Men's Committee have weekly prayer breakfasts at hundreds of locations throughout the nation. Besides the support of the prayer group, CBMC provides opportunities for evangelism and discipleship.

❑ Small groups are used for prayer, training, and evangelism by Search Ministries as it works with churches to increase the number of people involved in the harvest.

❑ Often groups form at individual worksites. Sometimes the effort is informal, with several Christians coming together during lunchtime for prayer and support. If the company permits, other groups are more formally publicized and structured. Worksite groups need to be careful to keep the effort focused on supporting outreach efforts of group members, instead of becoming an isolated Christian "club."

With the majority of women now working outside the home, their need for small group prayer and encouragement is often blocked by the obstacles of a tighter schedule and limited opportunities. My wife, Kathy, discovered that our church, like most others, held its only women's Bible study on a weekday, when most women now are at work. She felt God leading her to provide alternatives, so she assembled a leadership team to launch Women at Work, a small group ministry with meetings held both in the early morning and evening. Her breakfast group, originally scheduled for every other week, decided at their first meeting that they needed each other's prayer and support at least once a week.

The marketplace offers unlimited opportunities for us to fulfill our commission to go and make disciples. Our responsibility is to be prepared, to be available to others, and to be obedient to God's leading.

Think about It

❑ Are people open and interested in hearing about the Gospel from you? Where do you see opportunities for improvement in how you work, who you are, and what you say?

❑ How regularly are you praying for those with whom you work?

❑ How is your ministry support system? Do you have other

Christians to help you in terms of equipping, prayer, and encouragement or are you trying to fight the battle alone?

Notes

1. Bill Hybels, *Christians in the Marketplace* (Wheaton, Ill.: Victor Books, 1982), 32.

2. Doug Sherman and William Hendricks, *Keeping Your Ethical Edge Sharp* (Colorado Springs: NavPress, 1990), 174.

3. Doug Sherman and William Hendricks, *Your Work Matters to God* (Colorado Springs: NavPress, 1987), 242.

4. Frank R. Tillapaugh, *Unleashing the Church* (Ventura, Calif.: Regal Books, 1982), 202-3.

5. William E. Diehl, *The Monday Connection* (San Francisco: Harper San Francisco, 1991), 60.

6. Henry T. Blackaby and Claude V. King, *Experiencing God* (Nashville: Broadman & Holman Publishers, 1994), 78.

15

What Next?

W hen I finish reading a book, too often I say to myself, "Boy, there were some good ideas in there." Then I return the volume to the bookshelf and begin the process of forgetting most of what I just read.

After reading these pages, maybe you have been convicted by God to make your work a ministry. If so I offer the following steps as a means of applying the concepts from this book to your daily life. These six steps are meant to be a starting point; I am sure you will probably come up with many more to-do items on your own.

Step One

Pray to commit your work to God on a daily basis. At the start of each business day, offer up a prayer to God, committing each task you do to Him. Tell Him your intent to honor Him in all that you do. Pray for God's will to be done, in your life, at your workplace, and throughout the world.

> **Pray to commit your work to God on a daily basis.**

For me, the best time to commit my work to God is during the drive into work because I usually need to hit the ground running once I arrive. I also pray briefly before beginning large projects or tasks where I am on the hotseat, such as facilitating a meeting.

Step Two

Schedule a personal retreat to evaluate your working life. Spend a day or a weekend alone to prayerfully ponder your job and your career. If you dislike the work you currently do, working through the material covered in chapter 5 might be the logical place to start. Or you might evaluate your various job duties, seeing if they could be done in a manner more pleasing to God. Brainstorm how to become a better servant in your position or how to love coworkers more.

Each person's retreat will be different, depending on the issues he or she currently faces at work. The need for a retreat does not vary, however. Every time I step back from my work and reflect, God gives me additional new insights I can apply. I trust that your experience will be the same.

> **Schedule a personal retreat to evaluate your working life.**

Step Three

Commit to better equip yourself for your workplace ministry. If you and I are serious about making work our ministry, we quickly realize our shortcomings in carrying out that task. Perhaps our Bible knowledge is weak, or our job skills are no longer on the cutting edge, or we feel the need for more information about sharing our faith. When you have identified your area of need, make a commitment to take at least one step toward better equipping yourself each year, whether that step be a class, workshop, or independent study/reading. You'll be amazed at how God will use that new skill and knowledge.

> **Commit to better equip yourself for your workplace ministry.**

One area I've been working hard at improving is my computer skills. I was among the last of the business students trained without substantial use of computers (one computer course in seven years of higher learning). Marketing is now dominated by computers, with spreadsheet software for market research, database programs for marketing information systems, and desktop publishing systems for marketing communications. When I graduated from school, I was computer phobic. In recent years, I've clawed my way up toward mediocrity, but I still see many computer courses and tutorials in my future.

Step Four

Pray for those with whom you work. This step is absurdly simple to begin. Make a list of those with whom you interact at work and commit to praying through your list at least once a week. As you pray regularly for people, you'll notice people's needs more in day-to-day interactions with them. Ask God

> **Pray for those with whom you work.**

to let you know where and with whom you might serve in a more tangible way.

Step Five

Commit time to at least one work relationship for the coming year. Pray for God to help you identify a person you can make time for in your schedule. It may be a coworker, a vendor, or a neighbor. It may involve showing Christ's love to a troubled unbeliever or discipling a new Christian. Wherever God leads you, it is valuable to take the time to help someone else take another step forward in his or her spiritual journey.

> **Commit time to at least one work relationship for the coming year.**

I am grateful to the two men who took time to disciple me. Dave Rowe spent an hour a week with me for nearly four years of college. I had strayed in my walk with the Lord, and Dave helped give me a biblical foundation to get my life back on track. Years later, Bill John continued the discipling process by meeting me at 6 A.M. every Thursday morning for nearly two years. I can still turn to this mature Christian who knows me well enough to help.

What Next?

Step Six

Find or form a small group of Christians for prayer, encouragement, and accountability. Since this was discussed at the end of chapter 14, I won't repeat the details. All I know about small groups is that every significant spurt of spiritual growth I've ever experienced has occurred during a period when I've been involved in a small group experience.

> **Find or form a small group of Christians for prayer, encouragement, and accountability.**

In recent years we've seen our culture drift away from its Christian roots. One reason we as Christians have not been able to reverse the decline is that we are at our spiritual best on Sunday morning when the rest of the world doesn't see us. In reaching the marketplace for Christ, Monday morning must be the time when we shine brightly as we step out into a dark and needy world.

I pray that God will powerfully use you to light up your corner of the earth.

Think about It

❑ What ideas for change do you want to begin applying right away in your work?

Appendix
Questions for Group Discussion

If you are interested in using *Thank God It's Monday* in a small group or classroom setting, the following questions are included as a resource for generating meaningful discussion. Although each teacher has his or her own style, one approach for discussing each chapter is to:

❑ Give a brief overview of chapter content. Ask if anyone has any questions about the chapter or needs clarification.

❑ Ask group members to volunteer answers to the "Think about It" questions at the end of the chapter.

❑ Go through the discussion questions, relating back to chapter content as necessary.

❑ Ask group members' input to discuss ways they can apply the material in the chapter to their work.

Chapter One: A Marketplace That Needs God

1. What are some of the problems facing today's workplace? Make a list.

2. What obstacles are keeping the body of Christ from fully taking advantage of the opportunity in the workplace?

3. What are some ways that we as Christians can free ourselves from these limitations to better serve God in the marketplace?

Chapter Two: Expand Your Concept of Ministry

1. What kinds of activities do we normally think of when we hear the term *ministry?*

2. Read Colossians 3:17. Should there be a "secular" part to a Christian's life? Why or why not?

3. What are some advantages to seeing our work as ministry?

4. Using the biblical view of ministry, what kinds of ministry opportunities do we face on a regular basis on the job?

Chapter Three: Your Work Is God's Business

1. What does the Creation account—and the creation itself—teach us about God?

2. What can observing the work of God teach us about how we are to work?

3. In what ways might seeing God as our boss transform our work?

4. If we are supposed to be coworkers with God, how important is it to try to find out what God's will is? How do we seek God's will?

5. With God as our mentor, boss, and coworker, what kind of potential do Christians have to make an impact on the world?

Chapter Four: The Spiritual Benefits of Working in Business

1. In what ways does the curse show up in our work or workplaces? How can we limit its impact?

2. Read 1 Timothy 5:8. Why do you think Paul writes that one who does not provide for his family is worse than an unbeliever?

3. How should Christians compare with others in terms of the skillfulness of their work? In your opinion, how do they actually compare?

4. Read Philippians 2:4. What are some ways we can look out for the needs of others at work?

5. Read Ephesians 4:28. What kinds of things fall into the category of sharing with those in need?

6. How can we better make our daily toil an expression of our love for God?

Chapter Five: Seeing Business As a Calling

1. What is the impact of Christians not performing work consistent with their God-given abilities and interests?

2. What do you think of when you hear the term *calling?*

3. What are some ways we can discover our vocational calling from God?

4. How can we all become better stewards of the gifts and abilities God has given us?

5. Ask members of the group to share examples of seeking out work better suited to their gifts and abilities.

Chapter Six: Provide Good Service As God's Servants

1. How would providing good customer service impact our witness to others? What would be the impact of poor customer service?

2. What are some ways that workers can be more Christlike to their customers?

3. Why is listening to people and actually hearing what they have to say an important part of being a servant to them?

4. How do we build trust in business or other relationships when people have been let down so often in the past?

Chapter Seven: Love Your Coworker As Yourself

1. The Bible tells us to love our neighbor as ourselves. How do we do this with our 9 to 5 neighbors?

2. Why do many people treat those above them in the organization with more respect and kindness than those below them? How can we do a better job of treating all people with the same Christlike love?

3. Why do many managers find it so hard to compliment and so easy to criticize their employees? How can we improve our ability to praise others?

4. What can Christians (or the members of this group) do to ensure that we each pray for our coworkers and for opportunities to love them?

Chapter Eight: Work with Integrity and Honesty

1. Why is integrity so important in today's work setting?

2. What kind of little lies are accepted and commonplace on the job?

3. Frequently in the Old Testament, God condemns a "nickel and dime" theft practice of using two sets of weights and measures–generous ones for buying, skimpy for selling. What kinds of tiny theft opportunities present themselves each day at work?

4. How can we maintain our integrity when we will inevitably make mistakes and sin?

5. How can we help create an environment of integrity where we work?

Chapter Nine: Plan for the Long Haul

1. What are some advantages of having patience and persistence in the business world? How can we further develop these traits?

2. What are some of today's management fads? Why don't these fads and shortcuts last longer?

3. What are the challenges of maintaining a long-haul focus when working for a short-run organization or boss? How can we best overcome these problems?

4. How can we ensure that we allow enough flexibility in our planning to allow for God's leading?

Chapter Ten: Handling Tough Business Decisions

1. Is making a snap, decisive decision on a big issue a sign of wisdom? Why or why not?

2. What are some examples of big decisions that require careful research and godly insight?

3. Why are some of us hesitant in asking others for prayer and counsel in important matters?

4. Why is taking time to get away and "give thought to your ways" (Prov. 14:8) so important to sound decision-making?

Chapter Eleven: A Godly Approach to Success

1. What are some of the key differences between the world's standards of success and God's standards?

2. What dangers exist for those with too strong a desire for power and prestige?

3. Why do we so often catch ourselves seeking the approval of the world when the Bible teaches us that what the world values is "detestable" to God (Luke 16:15) and that the world will "hate" Christians? (John 15:19) Whose approval should we value?

4. Read 1 Timothy 6:9-10. What kind of "temptations" and "grief" can the love of money lead to?

5. In God's eyes, what does it take to be a successful Christian?

Chapter Twelve: Avoiding Work Addiction

1. What are some of the reasons why many of us work too much and rest too little?

2. Are there dangers or drawbacks to working too hard and not getting enough rest?

3. Why does God want us to rest?

4. Do we as Christians experience a Sabbath rest on Sundays? Why or Why not?

5. What are some ways that we can avoid work addiction and get more rest?

Chapter Thirteen: Entrepreneurs As Ministry Leaders

1. Do you think entrepreneurs have more freedom to live out their faith through their work than the average employee in a big corporation? Why or why not?

2. What are some good reasons for Christians to consider starting a business?

3. What are the pitfalls or potential risks in starting up a new venture?

Chapter Fourteen: Sharing Your Time and Your Faith

1. What kind of challenges do we face when witnessing in our workplace?

2. Read 1 Thessalonians 4:11-12, which says that good work will earn respect. Why is this important?

3. Read 1 Timothy 6:1-2. How should this passage affect how we treat those we work for?

4. How else can the way we work impact someone coming to know Christ?

5. Besides the Gospel message itself, how can what we say bring people closer to Christ?

6. How does a Christian know when the time is right to share the Gospel with another person? What do we need to do to be prepared for that moment?

7. Can you think of any additional ways to strengthen our workplace witness?

Chapter Fifteen: What Next?

1. What concepts presented in the book have been most useful to you in your work?

2. Has anyone begun implementing any changes since this group study began?

3. How can the members of this group help one another implement each of these steps?

4. What other action steps should we take to make our work a better ministry?